Michael,

Your great grandfather would have had an extraordinary time with you + your family.

XO

Dad

4 April

2012

Illustrated Catalogue Of The Valuable Paintings And Other Art Property: Recently Contained In The William Schaus Art Galleries, New York...sold...[jan. 15-17, 1912].

Hermann Schaus

ESTATE OF THE LATE HERMANN SCHAUS

THE VALUABLE PAINTINGS

AND OTHER ART PROPERTY

RECENTLY CONTAINED IN THE WELL-KNOWN

WILLIAM SCHAUS ART GALLERIES

AMERICAN ART GALLERIES

MADISON SQUARE SOUTH

NEW YORK

Schau

MAX

ON FREE PUBLIC VIEW
AT THE AMERICAN ART GALLERIES
MADISON SQUARE SOUTH, NEW YORK
BEGINNING WEDNESDAY, JANUARY 10TH, 1912

THE VALUABLE PAINTINGS

AND OTHER ART PROPERTY

BELONGING TO THE ESTATE OF THE LATE

HERMANN SCHAUS

OF NEW YORK

UNRESTRICTED PUBLIC SALE BY ORDER OF
THE EXECUTORS

ON MONDAY, TUESDAY, AND WEDNESDAY EVENINGS,
JANUARY 15TH, 16TH AND 17TH
BEGINNING EACH EVENING AT 8.00 O'CLOCK

IN THE GRAND BALL ROOM OF THE PLAZA

FIFTH AVENUE, 58TH TO 59TH STREETS

AND OTHER ART PROPERTY

RECENTLY CONTAINED IN THE

WILLIAM SCHAUS ART GALLERIES

FIFTH AVENUE, NEW YORK

TO BE SOLD AT

UNRESTRICTED PUBLIC SALE

BY ORDER OF MRS. SOPHIE J. SCHAUS, EXECUTRIX, AND
ADOLPHE SCHAUS, EXECUTOR, OF THE LATE

HERMANN SCHAUS

ON THE EVENINGS HEREIN STATED

IN THE GRAND BALL ROOM OF THE PLAZA

FIFTH AVENUE, 58TH TO 59TH STREETS

THE SALE WILL BE CONDUCTED BY
MR. THOMAS E. KIRBY, OF

THE AMERICAN ART ASSOCIATION, MANAGERS

NEW YORK

1912

S.G.

Press of THE LENT & GRAFF COMPANY
137-139 East 25th Street, New York.

CONDITIONS OF SALE

1. *The highest Bidder to be the Buyer, and if any dispute arises between two or more Bidders, the Lot so in dispute shall be immediately put up again and re-sold.*

2. *The Auctioneer reserves the right to reject any bid which is merely a nominal or fractional advance, and therefore, in his judgment, likely to affect the Sale injuriously.*

3. *The Purchasers to give their names and addresses, and to pay down a cash deposit, or the whole of the Purchase-money, if required, in default of which the Lot or Lots so purchased to be immediately put up again and re-sold.*

4. *The Lots to be taken away at the Buyer's Expense and Risk* within twenty-four hours from the conclusion of the Sale, unless otherwise specified by the Auctioneer or Managers previous to or at the time of Sale, *and the remainder of the Purchase-money to be absolutely paid, or otherwise settled for to the satisfaction of the Auctioneer, on or before delivery; in default of which the undersigned will not hold themselves responsible if the lots be lost, stolen, damaged, or destroyed, but they will be left at the sole risk of the purchaser.*

5. While the undersigned will not hold themselves responsible for the correctness of the description, genuineness, or authenticity of, or any fault or defect in, any Lot, and make no Warranty whatever, they will, upon receiving previous to date of Sale trustworthy expert opinion in writing that any Painting or other Work of Art is not what it is represented to be, use every effort on their part to furnish proof to the contrary; failing in which, the object or objects in question will be sold subject to the declaration of the aforesaid expert, he being liable to the Owner or Owners thereof for damage or injury occasioned thereby.

6. *To prevent inaccuracy in delivery, and inconvenience in the settlement of the Purchases, no Lot can, on any account, be removed during the Sale.*

7. *Upon failure to comply with the above conditions, the money deposited in part payment shall be forfeited; all Lots uncleared within one day from conclusion of Sale (unless otherwise specified as above) shall be re-sold by public or private sale, without further notice, and the deficiency (if any) attending such re-sale shall be made good by the defaulter at this Sale, together with all charges attending the same. This Condition is without prejudice to the right of the Auctioneer to enforce the contract made at this Sale, without such re-sale, if he thinks fit.*

8. *The Undersigned are in no manner connected with the business of the cartage or packing and shipping of purchases, and although they will afford to purchasers every facility for employing careful carriers and packers, they will not hold themselves responsible for the acts and charges of the parties engaged for such services.*

THE AMERICAN ART ASSOCIATION, MANAGERS.

THOMAS E. KIRBY, AUCTIONEER.

CATALOGUE

FIRST EVENING'S SALE

MONDAY, JANUARY 15TH, 1912

IN THE GRAND BALL ROOM OF THE PLAZA

FIFTH AVENUE, 58TH TO 59TH STREETS

BEGINNING AT 8 O'CLOCK

MLLE. ROSA MARIE BONHEUR .

FRENCH (1822-1899)

No. 79— CHEVAL ATTELÉ

PENCIL DRAWING

Height, 3¾ inches; length, 4¾ inches

THE drawing represents a sturdy cart-horse almost in profile, facing to the right. It is distinguished by its careful study of the harness, which includes a breast-band instead of a collar and a string of bells attached to the headgear.

Signed at the lower left, "ROSA B."

MLLE. ROSA MARIE BONHEUR

FRENCH (1822-1899)

No. 80— TOMBEREAU ATTELÉ D'UN CHEVAL

PENCIL DRAWING

Height, 5 inches; length, 9½ inches

THE drawing, made with pencil on white paper, presents a careful study of the side view of a Parisian trash-cart and of the horse's harness. The animal's head, which faces to the right, is indicated sketchily.

Signed at the lower left, "ROSA BONHEUR."

MLLE. ROSA MARIE BONHEUR

FRENCH (1822-1899)

No. 81— ### CHEVAL

PENCIL DRAWING

Height, 8½ inches; length, 12½ inches

EXECUTED on olive-toned paper with pencil and a few touches of white chalk, the study shows a racehorse, standing in profile to the right. While the near foreleg has been drawn a little back, the off one is a trifle advanced.

Signed at the lower left, "ROSA BONHEUR."

MLLE. ROSA MARIE BONHEUR

FRENCH (1822-1899)

No. 82— ### ÉTUDE: MARCHÉ AUX CHEVAUX

PENCIL DRAWING

Height, 5 inches; length, 12¾ inches

THE sketch, done in pencil on buff paper, seems to have been a study for *The Horse Fair*, now in the Metropolitan Museum. While it resembles the picture in general character it differs in several particulars. For example, the rearing stallion is being led by a man on foot, while the three horses at the right of the parade are not in the act of turning to the rear at a trot, but are shown in profile at a gallop.

Signed at the lower right, "ROSA B."

MLLE. ROSA MARIE BONHEUR

FRENCH (1822-1899)

No. 83—   VACHE

PENCIL DRAWING

Height, 11½ inches; length, 16 inches

THE pencil study on gray paper of a cow shows the body of the beast facing to the left, while the head is turned to the front. The horns are short and curve in to the eyes.

Signed at the lower left, "ROSA BONHEUR."

JOHN LEWIS BROWN

FRENCH (1829-1890)

No. 84—   STUDY OF HORSES

PENCIL AND WATERCOLOR

Height, 8½ inches; length, 11¼ inches

THE study is in pencil, washed over with sepia, white, vermillion and buff. At the left of the foreground a man, whose back is toward us, rests his elbow on the withers of a white horse. Over the latter's neck a brown horse, standing in the rear, lays his head. Parts of a third horse appear behind. At the right is a group of three figures; the center one reclining on the ground, while the others respectively stand and sit.

Signed at the lower right, "JOHN LEWIS BROWN."

ERNEST ALBERT MARKS

BRITISH (-1899)

No. 85—   BEACHED

WATERCOLOR

Height, 5¾ inches; length, 8½ inches

AN anchor lies at the left of the foreground of sand, which extends back to a horizontal strip of pale blue sea, ruffled with green, foamy surf.   Clear of the water lies a fishing-boat with a greenish hull and brown masts and rigging. Two figures, one of them distinguished by a red cap, are standing on the sand alongside.   Other boats, with sails spread, appear in the distance at the right.

Signed at the lower right, "ALBERT."

ERNEST ALBERT MARKS

BRITISH (-1899)

No. 86—   LOW TIDE

WATERCOLOR

Height, 5¾ inches; length, 8½ inches

THE greeny-gray sand, which occupies the foreground, is cut up into pools of whitish water and sprinkled with stones.   Some distance back a sailboat with green hull has been beached.   Beyond it, the water shows in a strip, feathered with sails.   There are indications, at the right, of a jetty, with a pole at its extremity, supporting a lantern.

Signed at the lower right, "ALBERT."

ERNEST ALBERT MARKS

BRITISH (-1899)

No. 87—   OUTWARD BOUND

WATERCOLOR

Height, 6 inches; length, 9½ inches

In the middle distance a steamer approaches, the water curling from her bow and smoke trailing aft. She carries two funnels and a square-rigged foremast, while the main and mizzen are bare. A bark appears in the distance at the right, while in the foreground at this side is a sailboat, containing a man in a blue jersey and another, distinguished by a red cap.

Signed at the lower left, "ALBERT."

J. H. LANGRAND

No. 88—   ROCKS AND WATER

WATERCOLOR

Height, 5¼ inches; length, 7½ inches

A RUGGED bit of shore, composed of dark, greenish, rocky formation, occupies the foreground, extending in an irregular diagonal from the lower right to some brown, scrubby trees which adjoin a yellowish headland far back at the left. The suggestion of a low spit of land and a few trees appears at the right of the horizon whence the greeny-blue water spreads smoothly toward the front. Slaty-blue clouds streak the lower sky, yielding above to gray-blue atmosphere.

Signed at the lower right, "J. H. LANGRAND."

GUISEPPE SIGNORINI

ITALIAN (1857-   )

No. 89—   A GOOD STORY

WATERCOLOR

Height, 12¾ inches; width, 9 inches

A CARDINAL, attired in rosy-crimson shovel hat, cassock and cloak (the last tied upon the chest with tasseled cords of gold tissue), stands reading a newspaper, his head inclined a little over his left shoulder, while a laugh plays about his lips. Behind him a flight of stone steps, flanked by a newel-post which is surmounted with a vase, leads up to a hedge of foliage with sharply defined leaves.

Signed at the lower right, "GUISEP. SIGNORINI, Paris, 14."

GUISEPPE SIGNORINI

ITALIAN (1857-   )

No. 90—   A VENETIAN

WATERCOLOR

Height, 12½ inches; width, 9½ inches

A VENETIAN magnifico of the sixteenth century is seated on an oak bench, against a wall that is embellished with two coats of arms, carved in yellow marble and let into gray marble panels. His left hand rests on the seat beside him while the right holds a large service book, bound in blue. His costume includes a pearly-drab and green satin damask robe, reaching to the feet. Its armholes reveal the sleeves of a doublet of crimson brocade, slashed and puffed with white at the elbows and shoulders.

Signed at the lower right, "GUISEP. SIGNORINI, Paris, 105."

ROBERT DE CUVILLON

FRENCH (1848-   )

No. 91—   HEAD OF A GIRL

WATERCOLOR

Height, 12 inches; width, 9½ inches

A GIRL's head and shoulders are posed three-quarters to the right; the left
shoulder being slightly depressed, as the head inclines over it. The bright,
gray eyes glance to the left, while a faint smile plays over the rosy lips. The
soft, brownish-blond hair, curling round the forehead, is dressed in the Greek
style with a fillet and arranged in a knot on the crown.

Signed and dated at the lower left, "R. DE CUVILLON, 1895, 210."

LUIGI LOIR

AUSTRIAN

No. 92—   VILLAGE LANDSCAPE

WATERCOLOR

Height, 9¾ inches; length, 14¼ inches

A WOMAN, accompanied by a child in a bright white pinafore, is passing along
the roadway, which crosses the foreground toward the left, where it is met by
another road at right angles. Along the latter a man and woman are approaching. This road is bounded on both sides by light green grass, the plot
at the right bearing a green apple tree and a bunch of trees smothered in
white blossoms. It is intersected by two paths which lead back to a barn distinguished by a long yellowish-brown roof, interrupted in the center by a gable.
Two poplars appear at the left of the barn and beyond them meadows extend
to distant hills.

Signed at the lower right, "LOIR LUIGI, No. 131."

GUISEPPE SIGNORINI

ITALIAN (1857-   )

No. 93—   A CAVALIER

WATERCOLOR

Height, 13½ inches; width, 10 inches

A GENTLEMAN, in the Court fashion of Henri II., stands facing the spectator, with arms folded, his rapier slung behind, so that the hilt and point are visible. His doublet and trunks of puce-colored material are trimmed with horizontal bars, between which are vertical tucks. His purple beaver has a narrow brim and a high crown, embellished with a white plume. A short violet mantle, lined with white, is fastened with gold tasseled cords below the ruff.

Signed at the lower right, "GUISEP. SIGNORINI, Paris."

BRUCE CRANE

AMERICAN (1857-   )

No. 94—   WINTER

WATERCOLOR

Height, 9¼ inches; length, 15¼ inches.

AN expanse of snow shows the indications of a roadway, starting near the center of the foreground and sweeping back in a curve to the left. Its course passes two willows, which stand on the right, and reaches a spinney of scrubby trees at the left of the middle distance. Violet woods show along the horizon, where a bar of saffron streaks the faint violet sky.

Signed at the lower right, "BRUCE CRANE."

CHARLES ÉDOUARD DE BEAUMONT

FRENCH (1821-   )

No. 95—   LADY WITH SWALLOW

WATERCOLOR

Height, 12 inches; width, 8 inches

WHILE a lady stands holding a swallow near her lips, a little child, in a pink dress, tied with a red sash and protected by a white pinafore, lifts up her hands to beg for it. The lady's figure, clad only in a blue skirt and chemisette bodice, cuts the line of a gilded console table, on which a vase stands.

Signed at the lower left, "E. DE BEAUMONT."

LUIGI CHIALIVA

ITALIAN (1842-   )

No. 96—   A PRISONER

WATERCOLOR

Height, 10 inches; length, 15½ inches

In an orchard, bounded at the back by apple trees and a barn, a woman is hammering a stake into the yellow-green turf, while a child holds the tether-cord of a nanny-goat. The mother wears a black dress and blue apron and a red kerchief wrapped round her head. The little one is dressed in a straw hat and pale blue pinafore. Beside the child appears a white kid, between which and the goat is another, marked with white and fawn.

Signed at lower left, "L. CHIALIVA."

PIERRE ÉDOUARD FRÈRE

FRENCH (1819-1886)

No. 97—   A FINISHING TOUCH

WATERCOLOR

Height, 14½ inches; width, 11¾ inches

As a girl and boy, each carrying a prayerbook, are starting for church, the boy leans forward, that his mother, seated at the right, may arrange his red tie. He wears a French schoolboy's cap and an olive-drab suit, while the little girl is dressed in a black hood and reddish-brown frock. The woman has a red kerchief over her head, her figure being clad in a pale blue jacket and still paler apron over a slaty skirt.

Signed and dated at the lower left, "EDOUARD FRERE, '85."

LUIGI LOIR

AUSTRIAN

No. 98—

RUE DU PORT, ST. CAST

WATERCOLOR

Height, 10½ inches; length, 13¾ inches

WHITE walls and pale lavender-pink roofs distinguish the cottages which border the village street and almost enclose its extremity. Sunflowers and greenery cluster against the wall of a house, taller than its neighbors, which is situated at the left of the foreground. In front of it two women, carrying a basket between them, are passing up the street behind a fisherman, who carries a net on his shoulder. Coming toward the front on the right, is a small boy in pale blue coat, wearing on his head a French sailor's blue cap with a red tuft in the center of the crown.

Signed at the lower right, "LOIR LUIGI, 118."

J. E. BUCKLEY

BRITISH

No. 99—

RETURNING FROM CHURCH

WATERCOLOR

Height, 10½ inches; length 16¼ inches

THE background presents a village church, with low ivy-covered spire and red-tiled nave, chancel and porch. It stands snugly among trees, in the midst of the graveyard, which is raised and surrounded by a retaining wall. The worshipers, costumed in the period of the second Charles, are defiling along the churchyard walk, descending the steps in the wall or passing along a horizontal path that leads to a timbered mansion at the right. Meanwhile, the lord of the manor, supporting his lady on his arm and accompanied by his little daughter, is coming toward the front.

Signed and dated at the lower left, "J. E. BUCKLEY, 1870."

ALPHONSE MARIE DE NEUVILLE

FRENCH (1836-1885)

No. 100—   FRENCH OFFICER

WATERCOLOR

Height, 16¼ inches; width, 12¼ inches

A FRENCH officer stands with feet apart, facing three-quarters to the right. His uniform comprises a lavender-pink cap; a bluish-black tunic, frogged and edged with fur; rose-colored breeches, with a black stripe down the seam, and reddish-brown boots, reaching above the knees. He is reading a despatch which he holds in his right hand, while the green envelope and a cigar are in his left. His horse appears at the left of the background in charge of a mounted orderly.

Signed and dated at the lower left, "A. DE NEUVILLE, 1882."

ALPHONSE MARIE DE NEUVILLE

FRENCH (1836-1885)

No. 101—   A GERMAN OFFICER

WATERCOLOR

Height, 19 inches; width, 12½ inches

A GERMAN officer stands facing three-quarters to the left, with legs stiffly close together. His uniform includes a slaty-colored cap, a purplish-drab tunic with yellow collar and cuffs, black breeches with a red stripe down the seam, and brown boots. A drab overcoat hangs loose from his shoulder. His left hand rests on the hilt of his sword, while the right holds a cigar.

Signed and dated at the lower right, "A. DE NEUVILLE, 1884."

G. BOURGAIN

FRENCH (CONTEMPORARY)

No. 102— ## L'ARRIVÉE DES RECRUES

WATERCOLOR

Height, 12½ inches; length, 20½ inches

THE scene presents the deck of a French battleship, on which seven recruits, in blue, double-breasted reefer jackets are lined up behind their kit bags. Three more occupy the rear file, toward which a fourth is hurrying, while the head and shoulders of another appear over the gangway ladder, at the top of which a sentry is stationed. A lieutenant stands in front of the recruits, checking off their names, and two other officers at the right of the foreground are watching the scene. In the harbor, at the left, is moored the training ship, an old frigate, from which a man-o'-war's boat is approaching.

Signed at the lower left, "G. BOURGAIN."

JULES DUPRÉ

FRENCH (1811-1889)

No. 103— ## AN OAK TREE

CRAYON DRAWING

Height, 17¼ inches; length, 20½ inches

THE composition involves a vigorous and truthful study of a European oak, with wide-spreading branches that are gnarled and angular and laden with tufts of thickly massed leaves. At the left and right of the foreground appear indications of scrubby bushes, while in the center there is a suggestion of a pool.

Signed at the lower left, "J. D."

JULES DUPRÉ

FRENCH (1811-1889)

No. 104— STUDY OF TREES

PENCIL

Height, 10¾ inches; length, 17 inches

THE study is made on buff paper with pencil and a little white chalk. Just left of the center stands an elm with branches and foliage bunched at the top of its straight trunk. Beside it is another with winding trunk that catches a little white light. Behind these trees are others, growing upon a knoll. At the right of the foreground stands a couple of trees whose stems curve over to the left.

Signed at the lower left, "J. D."

JULES DUPRÉ

FRENCH (1811-1889)

No. 105—   WILLOWS REFLECTED

CRAYON DRAWING

Height, 17¼ inches; length, 23 inches

AT the left of the composition, occupying some three-quarters of its width, four willows stand at the foot of a wooded slope. Their trunks and masses of soft foliage reappear reversed on the surface of a pool. Over the shadowed brow of an eminence at the right are seen the two dormer windows and roof of a house. The drawing is done with black crayon on a buff ground.

Signed at the lower right, "J. DUPRÉ."

WILLEM STEELINK

HOLLAND (1856-   )

No. 106—   SHEEP IN PASTURE

WATERCOLOR

Height, 17½ inches; width, 12½ inches

In the foreground a sheep stoops to drink from a pool, which straggles back with reedy banks toward the right. Another sheep stands with her head toward a farther group of four sheep, one of which is drinking. Behind the flock, at the left, is a mass of purplish-brown scrub, with sparse foliage, out of which grow two olive-drab trees, sprinkled with leaves, that show conspicuously in front of a woody clump. The horizon lies purple beneath a gray sky, shredded with olive vapor.

Signed above the lower left, "WILLEM STEELINK."

VICTOR BAUFFE

HOLLAND (1844-   )

No. 107—   MILL NEAR BLYCWYK

WATERCOLOR

Height, 13½ inches; length, 20½ inches

A PATH leads back across a dull green pasture, to a drab windmill which occupies the left of the middle distance. Two black and white cows appear nearer to the front, while beyond the mill stands a yellow rick, protected by a drab roof. At this point a stretch of land, marked with a distant windmill, extends to the right. It bounds the water which fills the right of the foreground. In the center of the latter a boat lies beside the bank, its occupant wearing a blue blouse. The sky is blurred with layers of gray cloud, broken up with a little white.

Signed at the lower right, "V. BAUFFE."

WILLEM CORNELIS RIP

HOLLAND (1856-   )

No. 108—   HERFSTAVOND NEAR GONDA

WATERCOLOR

Height, 13½ inches; length, 19½ inches

A YELLOW glow over the center of the horizon is reflected in the water which fills the foreground. A boat, occupied by a man in a dark blue blouse, lies near the right bank, where a woman, dressed in black, appears to be raking. Her white cap shows against the brown of a hedge, over the top of which is seen the bluish-white end of a cottage, with dark olive tawny thatch. Beside it stands a bare tree. Other bluish-white cottages and a windmill and trees interrupt the level sky line.

Signed at the lower right, "WILLEM RIP."

JOHN FR. HULK, JR.

HOLLAND (1855-   )

No. 109—   GEESE AND DUCKS

WATERCOLOR

Height, 12 inches; length, 19 inches

TOWARD the right of the foreground a white goose faces us while other geese and some ducks are disposed over the soft, olive-yellow grass. It extends back to a scrubby, brown hedge, interrupted by two rectangular patches of boarding, under one of which appears a goose. The hedge terminates at the left in a fence, constructed of purplish-blue boards and pickets. These are reflected in a pool of gray-white water, on which a duck is swimming.

Signed at the lower right, "JOHN F. HULK."

WILLEM STEELINK

HOLLAND (1856-   )

No. 110—   RETURN OF THE FLOCK

WATERCOLOR

Height, 12½ inches; length, 18 inches

A SINGLE sheep advances in the foreground, followed by a couple, behind which the flock fans out, their fleeces catching the light. The shepherd brings up the rear; his light blue blouse seen against the yellow-green grass of a slope which deepens to olive at the summit. At the right of the composition a tree trunk and scrubby bushes occupy a bank. In the distance slaty woods show beneath the rosy glow of the sky, which toward the zenith is a pale primrose.

Signed at the lower right, "WILLEM STEELINK."

WILLEM CORNELIS RIP

HOLLAND (1856-   )

No. 111—   ## MORNING NEAR GONDA

WATERCOLOR

Height, 8 inches; length, 14½ inches

WATER winds back irregularly through the center of the composition; while a polder, dotted with brown and white cows, extends at the left to a distant windmill. At the right, near the foreground, another mill stands beside a cottage. The latter has a reddish roof, that of the mill being slate, while the walls of both are olive-green. Off the bank lies a boat, which carries a mast and boom. A stooping figure appears in it, clad in a yellow oilskin.

Signed at the lower right, "WILLEM C. RIP."

HENRI HARPIGNIES

FRENCH (1819-   )

No. 112—   ## LANDSCAPE

WATERCOLOR

Height, 8 inches; length, 11 inches

IN the cool, even light of an almost white sky, three scrubby bushes, which extend across the foreground, show dark olive-green. A sandy road curves back through the center, disappearing behind a slope of ground which projects from the right. It is surmounted by two trees, one of which forks out from near the ground. At the left of the middle distance is a clump of grayish-buff and slaty-gray trees. Faint blue hills lie across the horizon.

Signed at the lower left, "H. HARPIGNIES."

JAN VAN ESSEN

HOLLAND (1854-   )

No. 113—   A WOODLAND POND

WATERCOLOR

Height, 13 inches; length, 18 inches

GREEN water winds back between soft, sedgy, yellow-green banks, until it becomes blue and white in the distance. Here it is bounded by a belt of wood. At the right of the pond, near the foreground, a young tree, with yellow pointed leaves, shows against a dense brown thicket. The opposite bank is studded with saplings; the yellow leaves with which they are sprinkled being round. Under one of them lie some white ducks with their heads tucked beneath their wings.

Signed and dated at the lower right, "JAN VAN ESSEN, 1904."

PAUL JEAN CLAYS

FLEMISH (1819-1900)

No. 114—   CALME SUR L'ESCAUT

WATERCOLOR

Height, 17¼ inches; width, 11½ inches

Two GULLS hover over the water in the foreground, one of them above the reflections cast by two sailing barges, side by side in the center of the composition. The left-hand one shows a band of apple-green above the dull red of her bow, while a blue pennon floats from her masthead. The other is distinguished by a red mainsail and pale tawny-yellow topsail and jib. Other shipping appears in the background, while on a horizontal strip of land in the left distance stands a tall lighthouse.

Signed and dated at the lower right, "P. J. CLAYS, 1878."

JOSEF ISRAËLS

HOLLAND (1824-1911)

No. 115—   MOTHER AND BABY

WATERCOLOR

Height, 8⅜ inches; width, 5⅜ inches

A YOUNG mother, with her baby on her lap, is engaged in sewing. Her figure is shown in profile, facing to the left, the white cap being silhouetted against the fresh green of a landscape, seen through a window. The baby leans against her bosom, with one little hand laid on her left arm. The mother is dressed in a bluish waist, with short sleeves, and a brown skirt.

Signed at the lower left, "JOSEF ISRAELS."

JOSEF ISRAËLS

HOLLAND (1824-1911)

No. 116—   WASHING DAY

WATERCOLOR

Height, 12¾ inches; width, 7¾ inches

THE scene presents the angle, included by two brown walls of a humble kitchen, paved with reddish tiles. The right-hand wall is interrupted by two strings of onions and by what appears to be a niche. Through a window in the left wall a pale green landscape is visible. Its lower right corner is cut by the head of a woman who stands over a steaming washtub. The latter is brown as well as the stand which supports it. The woman's skirt is dark brown, with a touch of blue on the hip, while her waist is pinkish-brown. The tonality is impregnated with dim atmosphere.

Signed at the lower left, "JOSEF ISRAËLS."

JOHAN BARTHOLD JONGKIND

HOLLAND (1819-1891)

No. 117— WINTER IN HOLLAND

WATERCOLOR

Height, 6 inches; length, 10 inches

THE picture is executed in crayon, washed over with water color. From the foreground a canal extends back in the center of the composition, frozen over with purplish-blue ice. A boy is skating forward behind a man, whose costume shows a touch of brown, as he skates beside a little girl, dressed in pale green. On the bank at the left of the foreground stands a clump of brown trees, adjoining a cottage, beyond which rises a windmill.

Signed at the lower right, "JONGKIND."

JOHAN HENDRIK VAN MASTENBROEK

HOLLAND (1875-   )

No. 118—   VIEW OF ROTTERDAM

WATERCOLOR

Height, 14 inches; width, 11 inches

A QUAY extends back from the left of the foreground. It is bordered by a line of olive-brown trees and a lamp post, beyond which appears a row of dull red houses with white casements. Figures dot the quay near two empty push-carts. Alongside the canal wall lies a barge, with its stern that shows a bright green band round the gunwale, turned to the spectator. Smoke rises from the cabin smokestack, and the upper part of a man in a pale blue blouse is seen beyond it.

Signed and dated at the lower left, "J. H. V. MASTENBROEK, '98."

JAKOB MARIS

HOLLAND (1837-1899)

No. 119—   A VIEW OF DELFT

WATERCOLOR

Height, 13¼ inches; length, 15¾ inches

A TRIANGLE of shore appears at the right of the foreground, the rest of which is filled with the water of a canal that stretches back diagonally to a windmill, faintly visible toward the extreme right of the horizon. Another windmill shows prominently at the end of a quay which borders the farther side of the canal. The low houses, clustering along it, have dull red roofs, save in the center of the picture where a building is distinguished by a roof of pinkish tiles. Over its top in the distance rises a third windmill. A dark hulled boat, flying a blue pennon at her mast, lies moored toward the left of the quay.

Signed at the lower right, "J. MARIS."
Collection the Right Hon. Sir J. C. Day.

PAUL JEAN CLAYS

FLEMISH (1819-1900)

No. 120— AMSTERDAM

WATERCOLOR

Height, 11¼ inches; length, 17¼ inches

THE water of the harbor is dyed with whitish-gray of a sky that shows a little bright blue at the zenith. With this is mingled the rich reflections of the sails of the fishing fleet. A boat at the right, which has some slaty-blue on her gunwale, is rigged with a mainsail, topsail and jib of warm, tawny buff. Another at the left has a lavender-pink mainsail, while the rest of her canvas is of brownish color. Purplish-brown and slaty-gray hues distinguish a third.

Signed at the lower right, "P. J. CLAYS."

JOHN FR. HULK, JR.

HOLLAND (1855-   )

No. 121—   A SETTER

WATERCOLOR

Height, 11½ inches; length, 18½ inches

A SETTER stands across the foreground, pointing to the left, with left fore-
paw raised and head, back and tail in horizontal tension. The white of his
coat is interrupted by liver-colored ears and by small patches of the same
hue on the back and at the root of the tail. The background at the right is
filled in with a mass of oak foliage, dyed red and yellow, while at the left
appears a knoll, crowned by a thicket of young tree stems.

Signed at the lower right, "JOHN F. HULK."

WILLEM CORNELIS RIP

HOLLAND (1856-   )

No. 122—   MOLENS ON THE LEK

WATERCOLOR

Height, 13½ inches; length, 19½ inches

THE end of a raft of floating planks projects from the front, at the right
of the water which extends across the foreground and back to a low horizon.
On the right bank two windmills, the nearer of which shows a touch of dark
blue on its hood, rise above a cluster of cottages with reddish brown roofs.
Off the wharf in front of them are moored a red and a purplish-red barge.
In the center of the canal lies a boat with a tawny-buff sail and a patch of
green on her hull.

Signed at the lower right, "WILLEM RIP."

WILLEM STEELINK

HOLLAND (1856-   )

No. 123—   SHEEP RETURNING HOME

WATERCOLOR

Height, 19 inches; width, 14 inches

BEECH trunks border the sandy path which leads up from the center of the foreground to a skyline, sloping down from right to left. Here the figure of the shepherd, as far as the waist, appears above the packed mass of his flock. The sheep are coming down the incline, headed by two which move side by side. The wood is carpeted with red and yellow leaves, shed by the trees which wear their autumnal tints.

Signed above the lower right, "WILLEM STEELINK."

MARIA PHILIPPINE VAN BOSSE BILDERS

HOLLAND (1837-1900)

No. 124—   LANDSCAPE

WATERCOLOR

Height, 13½ inches; length, 20¾ inches

BETWEEN strips of gray-green mossy grass a small canal stretches back from the front and joins a larger one which crosses the composition horizontally. A willow stands in the water near the foreground, and farther back at the junction of the two waterways rises a square wooden tower, apparently a lighthouse. At the right of it a sail and the upper part of two men appear above the bank of the main channel. The latter is bounded at the far side by purplish-brown woods and occasional cottages, over which soar masses of gray and white vapor, showing intervals of atmospheric blue.

Signed at the lower left, "M. BILDERS VAN BOSSE."

JOHAN HENDRIK VAN MASTENBROEK

HOLLAND (1875-   )

No. 125—   A WHARFSIDE

WATERCOLOR

Height, 13½ inches; length, 21½ inches

A SCREEN of bare brown trees, through which houses are visible, stands high up at the left of the composition. A brown bank slopes irregularly down from it to the water which fills the right of the scene. Two figures appear in the shadow of the bank near the foreground, while the cream and drab and light blue blouses of some workmen catch the light. They are grouped near a shed, in front of which a wharf projects, with barges moored at its extremity. Beyond the wharf is visible the funnel of a steamer, distinguished by a white band on a black ground. A sister steamer lies horizontally across the water in the right distance.

Signed and dated at the lower left, "J. H. V. MASTENBROEK, '99."

WILLEM CORNELIS RIP

HOLLAND (1856-   )

No. 126—   ON THE RHINE NEAR LIENDEN

WATERCOLOR

Height, 14½ inches; length, 21 inches

ALONG a road which crosses the composition diagonally from the left of the foreground a countryman in blue blouse is riding a white farm horse. He is approaching a cottage with bluish-white walls and dark olive-tawny thatch, which nestles below the level of the road upon the edge of a river at the left. Close behind the cottage towers a windmill. At this point the road disappears, and on the right a church spire projects above a clump of mossy-green trees.

Signed at the lower left, "WILLEM RIP."

JOHN FR. HULK

HOLLAND (1855-   )

No. 127— GEESE IN A SWAMP

WATERCOLOR

Height, 15¼ inches; length, 24½ inches

THE water in the marshy foreground is cut into with grassy growth, the gray-green of which is pricked with a few white flowers. Stepping forward on a spit of grass is a white goose, beyond which appear two others, one of them lowering its head to feed. Under the lee of a mass of bulrushes at the right of the middle distance appears a group of geese. In the distance yellowish polders, dotted with cattle, extend to slaty-purple hills, which lie across a high horizon beneath a violet-gray sky.

Signed and dated at the lower left, "JOHN F. HULK, 1907."

VICTOR BAUFFE

HOLLAND (1849-   )

No. 128— A HOLLAND LANDSCAPE

WATERCOLOR

Height, 14½ inches; length, 21½ inches

THE left of the foreground is occupied with water, which extends back to a horizontal bank and passes to the right. In the meadow, thus enclosed at the right, is a clump of willows, to two of which a pole is fixed. Upon this hang some garments, while a woman stoops to spread some linen on the grass. She wears a white cap, old rose waist, blue apron and brown skirt. Seen across the water behind her is a little church. Farther to the left stand two brown cottages with olive thatch. A boat with brown sails appears at the left of the water.

Signed at the lower right, "V. BAUFFE."

JAN VAN VUUREN

HOLLAND (1871-   )

No. 129—   ENTRANCE TO THE WOOD

WATERCOLOR

Height, 16 inches; length, 20 inches

THE foreground is in shadow, interrupted by a couple of white posts at the foot of a slight knoll on the right, from which rise two beech trunks. Beyond the latter appears a purplish-brown roof. At the left of the middle distance a brown hut stands beside a thatched cottage, whose white wall catches the light. The latter also illumines the patch of ground in front of the cottage and glistens between the trunks of a grove of beech trees in the background. The foliage is yellowing with the approach of Fall.

Signed and dated at the lower right, "J. VAN VUUREN, 1900."

JOHN FR. HULK, JR.

HOLLAND (1855-   )

No. 130—   DUCK HUNTING

WATERCOLOR

Height, 16 inches; length, 24½ inches

SHELTERED by a mass of bulrushes, a brown boat projects from the right. Standing in its high sharp bow and pointing, is a white setter with orange-tawny markings on the ears and back. A man in a dark olive coat sits behind the dog, while another, dressed in a blue blouse, stands leaning forward, as if to steady the boat. The various colors are reflected in the purplish-blue water. Two ducks are flying in the slaty-gray sky.

Signed at the lower right, "JOHN F. HULK."

WILLEM CORNELIS RIP

HOLLAND (1856-   )

No. 131—   VIEW ON THE SCHIE

WATERCOLOR

Height, 14½ inches; length, 25¼ inches

A WINDMILL of brownish plum color, surmounting the dark red roof of an octagonal structure with drab walls and a blue door, stands a little back from the foreground at the right. The interval is encumbered with planks and logs, floating in an arm of the canal, which itself extends back at the left. Several brown boats are scattered over the foreground; one of them, in which a man in plum-colored blouse is seated, showing bits of deep green cargo. The water is purplish-blue with the whitish reflections of a pale weathery sky.

Signed at the lower right, "W. RIP."

GUISEPPE SIGNORINI

ITALIAN (1857-   )

No. 132—   DANS LA BIBLIOTHÈQUE

WATERCOLOR

Height, 16¾ inches; length, 22¼ inches

A BOOKCASE of rococo design, decorated with a festoon of carved and gilded flowers, occupies the background. In front of it is a table, covered with a silvery-blue velvet cloth, embroidered with silver. At the right of it a young lady sits in profile, reading. Pink ostrich plumes adorn her blond hair, while her figure is elegantly attired in a pompadour skirt of pearly-gray with dainty rose stripes enclosing floral sprays, over a petticoat of alternate bands of rosy cream and pale olive-blue, sprinkled with little flowers. Resting his elbow on the left side of the table, an old gentleman in a magenta-colored costume sits listening to the story.

Signed at the lower right, "GUISEP. SIGNORINI, Paris, 262."

BERNARDUS JOHANNES BLOMMERS

HOLLAND (1845-   )

No. 133—   MINDING BABY

WATERCOLOR

Height, 16 inches; length, 20¼ inches

A WICKER cradle, draped over the hood with a black and gray shawl, occupies the center of the composition. The pink-faced baby is lifting its left hand to the young mother, as she stands at the right watching it. Her figure is seen in profile, the back bent forward, the hands resting on the knees. In the rear of the scene appears a large fireplace, paneled at the side with blue and white tiles, while a blue bureau stands at the left, with a row of three plates leaning against the wall.

Signed at the lower right, "BLOMMERS."

JOHAN HENDRIK VAN MASTENBROEK

HOLLAND (1865-   )

No. 134—   SUNSET

WATERCOLOR

Height, 19 inches; length, 28½ inches

THE water stretches from the front to a low horizon, fringed with purple woods. Over the center of these the sun's half-orb shows yellow under level strata of purplish-orange cloud, surmounted by a confused mass of darkening vapor. Along the left of the canal extends a quay on which appear a clump of trees and some red-roofed houses; while across the water spreads a mossy-green pasture. Two boats lie off the bank, in one of which stands a man with a pole.

Signed and dated at the lower right, "J. H. V. MASTENBROEK, 1905."

WILLEM MARIS

HOLLAND (1844-1910)

No. 135—   DUCKS AND DUCKLINGS

WATERCOLOR

Height, 14½ inches; length, 23½ inches

THE scene presents a spot of bright green grass in front of a little pond, the surface of which is boldly dappled with light and shade, under branches clothed with long yellowish leaves. Six yellow ducklings are sprinkled near a white duck, who is preening her feathers. At her left stands another white one, while at the right a bluish duck is lying beside a yellowish-brown one with scarlet on her head.

Signed at the lower right, "WILLEM MARIS."

WILLEM STEELINK

HOLLAND (1856-   )

No. 136—

SHEEP ON THE HEATH

WATERCOLOR

Height, 15 inches; length, 25¼ inches

OVER the d r a b foreground, scantily spotted with short herbage, the sheep are spread in a fan, the point of which is toward t h e spectator. The shepherd, in blue blouse and brown trousers, stands at the left of his flock, propped upon his stick, the upper part of h i s body showing against the horizontal line of a scrubby, bare hedge. The latter terminates at the center of the composition in three almost leafless trees, to the right of which extends the dark, olive-buff-black mass of a long thatched roof. Over the top of it appear three posts of a rick roof.

Signed at the lower right, "WILLEM STEELINK."

JOHAN HENDRIK VAN MASTENBROEK

HOLLAND (1875-   )

No. 137—   MORNING FROST

Height, 19¼ inches; length, 28½ inches

ABOVE the horizontal line of trees which bounds the view of the harbor, the sun glimmers white in the dove-gray vapory sky, and trails its reflection over the water to the front. At the left of the latter five rowboats, containing fishermen, are sprinkled in a group. A laden barge is being towed by a tug toward a wharf in the middle distance at the right. Beyond the wharf extends a row of houses. A man operating a pole, stands in the stern of a barge, which has a rowboat with a single occupant in tow.

Signed and dated at the lower right, "J. H. V. MASTENBROEK, 1904."

FRANÇOIS PIETER TER MEULEN

HOLLAND (1843-   )

No. 138—   A SHEPHERDESS

WATERCOLOR

Height, 27½ inches; width, 21 inches

A ROSY-FACED girl is knitting as she sits on a bank, in profile to the left. Yellow leaves are strewn around her and a sapling, from which the top is broken, shows at her back. In the distance, at the left, is a thicket of young trees amid which the flock is feeding, while a sheep and a lamb appear in the middle distance. The girl is dressed in a white cap and blue apron that reaches from her neck to her feet.

Signed at the lower left, "F. P. TER MEULEN."

WILLEM CORNELIS RIP

HOLLAND (1856-   )

No. 139—   MOLENS NEAR ZEVENHUYOEN

WATERCOLOR

Height, 19½ inches; length, 28½ inches

ON a road that winds through the center of the foreground a cart approaches, with a white horse in the shafts. The driver wears a dark blue blouse. The road leads back to a mill, which is seen across a sheet of water that occupies the left of the foreground. Under the far bank appears a punt, containing a man in a blue blouse. In the distance on this side are seen four windmills, and another overtops a cluster of brown roofs at the right.

Signed at the lower left, "WILLEM RIP."

FRITZ THAULOW

NORWEGIAN (1847-1906)

No. 140—   DEGEL—NORWAY

PASTEL

Height, 19¾ inches; length, 29¼ inches

A FEW stars show in the blue sky, but the village street is wrapt in gloom. The snow on the roofs of the cottages along the right is a vague gray-blue, and the drab walls pierced with the rosy, creamy light from four windows and a transom, glimmer uncertainly. Before a dark doorway a man and a woman stand conversing. Out in the roadway, where the glare from the windows is reflected in some puddles, a man comes forward with his hands in his pockets, followed by a girl leading a child. At the left of the roadway stands a row of poplars.

*Signed at the lower right, "*FRITZ THAULOW.*"*

GUISEPPE SIGNORINI

ITALIAN (1857-   )

No. 141—   UNE FEMME PEINTRE

WATERCOLOR

Height, 18 inches; length, 23 inches

AT the right of an easel, whose edge occupies almost the center of the composition, a young lady leans forward on her seat, diligently painting. She is elegantly attired in a gown of pale blue damask, besprinkled with purple, golden yellow and rosy blossoms, down the front of which descends a panel of pearly-gray with an arabesque design in gold, rose, green and blue. Her subject is seated at the left of the easel—an oldish gentleman, whose knees embrace a large *chaufferette*. Above his head hangs a picture of two loves, while on the wall behind the lady is a series of panels, each containing the figure of a saint.

Signed at the lower right, "GUISEP. SIGNORINI, Paris, 262."

GUISEPPE SIGNORINI

ITALIAN (1857-   )

No. 142—   RETOUCHE DU PROFESSEUR

WATERCOLOR

Height, 18¾ inches; length, 24½ inches

THE profile of an easel divides the composition about the center. At the right an old gentleman, facing the spectator, sits posing for his portrait. Meanwhile, on the other side of the easel, the lady-artist has yielded her chair to a young professor, and leans on the back of it as she watches the process of retouching. Her gown is of pale blue satin, trimmed with silver embroidery, while the young man's costume consists of a white tie-wig, crimson, gold-bedecked coat and breeches and scarlet stockings.

Signed at the lower right, "GUISEP. SIGNORINI, Paris, 266."

PIERRE J. PELLETIER

FRENCH

No. 143—   LA FOLIE NANTELLE

PASTEL

Height, 20 inches; length, 29¾ inches

FROM the foreground a roadway leads back to the greenish-blue door of a drab house, the roof of which is fantastically embellished with red coping tiles and a number of red chimney pots. A woman approaches the door. At the left of the roadway is a stretch of sandy earth, strewn with stones and bordered by a mossy wall, over the top of which shows a row of trees. On a bank at the right of the foreground stands the dark gable end of a house, surmounted by a high chimney and light red roof.

Signed at the lower right, "PELLETIER."

LUIGI CHIALIVA

ITALIAN (1842-   )

No. 144—   SPRING LANDSCAPE

WATERCOLOR

Height, 15 inches; length, 21½ inches

THE pasture slopes up from the foreground, having at the right of the summit a group of straggling young peach trees, laden with pink and white blossoms. A shepherdess is seated on the left of the slope, clasping her knees with folded hands as she watches three lambs which stand in advance of the sheep. The rest of the flock is grouped at the right, where the sheep-dog stands on the alert, with quivering tongue hanging out. The girl wears a reddish-purple handkerchief around her head and a pinkish-brown dress with a creamy-drab tippet over the shoulders. An umbrella lies by her side.

Signed at the lower left, "L. CHIALIVA."

AUGUST FRANZEN, A. N. A.

AMERICAN (1868-   )

No. 145—   CALLING ON THE SQUIRE

WATERCOLOR

Height, 20¼ inches; width, 13¼ inches

In a garden, gay with flowers, a gentleman with gray hair and beard, sits sideways on a green bench. He rests his head on his hand, as he faces a young man and woman seated at the left. The youth wears a white yachting cap and scarlet tie and holds his hand on the back of his chair with a cigarette between the fingers. His companion is dressed in a blue hat, yellow waist, and rose and buff figured skirt.

Signed at the lower right, "FRANZEN."

GUISEPPE SIGNORINI

ITALIAN (1857-   )

No. 146—   RICHE ARABE DANS SON FUMOIR

WATERCOLOR

Height, 27 inches; width, 20 inches

A BLACK-BEARDED Arab is seated on a bench, holding his long pipe unsmoked, while he leans against the green and gray tiled wall in an attitude of reverie. At his side is a tabouret with sweetmeat box and coffee cup, and behind it stands a Nubian slave in a long, plain yellow silk tunic, elevating a perforated brass sphere from which fragrant smoke-wreaths issue. The gentleman's garb comprises a rosy-crimson jacket, embroidered, like the yellow vest, with silver, and crimson-damask trousers; a salmon-pink drapery being laid over his pale blue turban.

Signed at the lower right, "GUISEP. SIGNORINI, Paris, 305."

PIERRE J. PELLETIER

FRENCH

No. 147—   BILLANCOURT

PASTEL

Height, 22 inches; length, 36 inches

In the paling light of a stormy sky a roadway extends from the foreground toward the left. Here two carts interrupt its monotony. Near the sidewalk stands a telegraph post, the wires cutting the sky diagonally. Then appears a lamp-post, past which two women are walking. On the opposite sidewalk, two women stand in conversation, and a man, carrying a basket, is hurrying along beside a woman who holds a child by the hand. The walk is bounded by a wall, over which appear the roofs of two sheds and a couple of house-boats, with a view of the river beyond, reaching back to a factory and smokestack in the left distance.

Signed at the lower left, "J. Pelletier."

ALBERT LOREY GROLL, A. N. A.

AMERICAN (1866-   )

No. 148—   THE DESERT

PASTEL

Height, 21 inches; length, 33½ inches

The level of the desert is interrupted near the foreground at the left by an eminence that rises to its highest point by successive undulations. This almost wave-line formation is swept with tones of purple, orange, green and cream. The desert, yellow-green and studded with sage-brush in the middle distance, pales to cream as it approaches a blue and rosy mountainous barrier on the horizon. Its contours, partly rounded, partly serrated, show against a pale blue sky, in which soar two conspicuous white clouds with ragged edges.

Signed at the lower right, "A. L. Groll."

GUISEPPE SIGNORINI

ITALIAN (1857-   )

No. 149—   MARCHAND DE CURIOSITÉS

WATERCOLOR

Height, 30½ inches; width, 19 inches

An Arab, swathed in crimson, with a rosy, crimson hat slung at his back, stands offering for sale an instrument which has two rows of eight strings, strained over a kettle-drum body, covered with sheepskin. A gray-bearded merchant, seated on the floor beside some brass lamps, a brass dish embossed with a horse and rider, a tabouret, inlaid with mother-of-pearl, and other articles, is passing his left hand over the body of the instrument. An almost feminine elegance distinguishes the old man's costume which comprises a crimson turban, pink silver-embroidered robe, yellow vest and a drapery shawl of yellow, crimson and blue stripes.

Signed at the lower right, "GUISEP. SIGNORINI, Paris, 294."

CONSTANT BROCHART

FRENCH

No. 150—   MAUD MULLER

PASTEL

Height, 47½ inches; width, 32½ inches

A YOUNG girl, holding the handle of a rake with one hand and a tin mug in the other, sits beside a runnel of water. Her straw hat is trimmed with pinkish-brown ribbon and decked with marguerites and poppies. Round her neck lies a silk handkerchief of old rose, gray and light blue plaid; while her white chemisette is confined by a black bodice, above a blue skirt, turned up and bunched over the hips.

Signed on a stone at the lower right, "CONSTANT BROCHART."

PIERRE J. PELLETIER

FRENCH

No. 151—   ISSY LES MOULINEUX

PASTEL

Height, 22½ inches; length, 35½ inches

FROM the left of the foreground a street stretches back to the center of the middle distance, while a roadway descends to the riverside at the right. Here there is a wharf, heaped with sand, with a black barge moored alongside. The water extends back to where two red roofs and a f a c t o r y chimney show against a sky filled with rain-clouds. The sidewalk at the left of the street is bordered with a paling, over the top of which appear a tree and the brick walls and brown roofs of houses. A lady in red dress walks beside a man.

*Signed at the lower right, "*J. PELLETIER*."*

GUISEPPE SIGNORINI

ITALIAN (1857-   )

No. 152—   ANTICHAMBRE DU HAREM

WATERCOLOR

Height, 34 inches; width, 22¾ inches

A BRASS lamp hangs above a large bowl, from which fans out a profusion of pampas blossom, the plumes on the left spreading across a Moorish-Gothic grille. Beneath this display appear a standing and a seated musician. The latter, distinguished by a handsome pink silk drapery, the lining of which is embroidered in silver and pale-olive green, rests his foot on a tabouret, while he sings to the accompaniment of a lute-shaped instrument. His companion, whose crimson robe reveals the apple-green velvet sleeves of a jacket, is drawing a bow across the two strings of an instrument consisting of a very small circular body and long slender neck.

*Signed at the lower right, "*GUISEP. SIGNORINI, Paris, 301*."*

GUISEPPE SIGNORINI

ITALIAN (1857-   )

No. 153—   DOGE DE VENISE

WATERCOLOR

Height, 49½ inches; width, 29½ inches

A MAN, superbly costumed, stands facing the spectator, his left hand grasping a rolled document, while his right turns the illuminated page of a large book, supported on a revolving desk. His figure is enveloped in the voluminous folds of a rose silk robe, over which descends from his right shoulder a broad stole of cream and purplish-red brocade. Two men, similarly attired, are seated in the shadow of the background, against an oak-paneled wall. The scene represents the interior of the Hall of the Council of Ten.

Signed at the lower right, "GUISEP. SIGNORINI."

SECOND EVENING'S SALE

TUESDAY, JANUARY 16TH, 1912

IN THE GRAND BALL ROOM OF THE PLAZA

FIFTH AVENUE, 58TH TO 59TH STREETS

BEGINNING AT 8 O'CLOCK

JULES ALEXIS MEUNIER

FRENCH

Contemporary

No. 154—FISHERMEN ON THE EDGE OF THE QUAY

PANEL

Height, 6 inches; length, 9¼ inches

THE quay extends back from the left of the foreground, rosy-white in the sunshine. Near the front two fishermen are seated on the edge, their feet dangling over the water. The nearer one, an old man in brown cap and a slaty-drab coat, leans forward with his hands on his knees, while his companion turns to him, mouth open, gesticulating. Facing the men are the bows of three boats, which project horizontally from the right with a diminishing amount of the hull in view. The one most in sight is painted pale green, the next darker green, with "Villefranche" lettered on the gunwale, while the last is white; the colors of all being reflected in the mauve water.

Signed at the lower left, "J. A. MEUNIER."

H. BRELING

GERMAN

No. 155—   RIDING PILLION

PANEL

Height, 6 inches; width, 4 inches

A WHITE horse has one foreleg raised in the act of stepping out of a narrow stream that it has forded. It is mounted by a man in a buff tunic and brown boots with flaps reaching above the knees. With her right arm round his waist, a woman rides behind him, pillion fashion. She wears an old-rose jacket, drawn in at the waist. A chateau, with a round tower at one of the angles of its outer wall, shows in the distance at the left.

Signed and dated, "H. BRELING, 1887."

LUIGI LOIR

AUSTRIAN

No. 156—   A PARIS STREET—EVENING

PANEL

IN the waning light the roadway, which extends back from the foreground, is damp with rain. The sky is heavy with dull drab vapor, gathered over a glaring white horizon, against which show the umbrellas of passengers on the top of an omnibus. It has halted beside a *boutique* for tickets, situated at the left on the sidewalk, where also appear a lamp post and newspaper kiosk. On the opposite side of the street yellow lights flare in the shop windows. A cart, drawn by a white horse, is coming down the street, followed by a hansom. Walking toward them from the right of the foreground is a boy in white apron, coat and cap, carrying a red can.

Signed at the lower right, "LOIR, LUIGI."

LUIGI LOIR

AUSTRIAN

No. 157—　　　　THE HARBOR—NIGHT

PANEL

THE foreground shows a triangle of drab-colored roadway with a strip of pale green grass that separates it from a reversed triangle of slaty-purple water. On the latter lies a houseboat with two windows, glowing red; beyond which the horizon line is interrupted by a puff of smoke and dotted with yellow lights. A green light glimmers at the top of a pole beside a building in the middle distance at the right, from which a wharf projects. A carriage, with lighted lamps, and three female figures spot the road.

Signed at the lower right, "LOIR, LUIGI."

SIEKERZ SZYKIER

POLISH

No. 158—　　　　WINTER

PANEL

Height, 9½ inches; width 7 inches

SNOW, shaded with bluish-gray, covers the scene, which in the foreground presents the summit of a slight hill. The top has just been reached by a black horse, advancing at a gallop. His head is encircled with a large horse-shoe yoke, attached to the shafts of a sleigh. The latter is being driven by a woman, who stands leaning back on the reins. She is dressed in a plum-red jacket and reddish-brown skirt, while a dark kerchief surrounds her plump, smiling face. Another face appears in the bottom of the sleigh. Close behind follows a second sleigh, drawn by a white horse in charge of a man.

Signed and dated at the lower left, "SZYKIER SIEKERZ, Munachium, 1890."

H. BRELING

GERMAN

No. 159—   THE PRISONER

PANEL

Height, 5 inches; length, 6 inches

In front of the gabled end of a thatched cabin at the left of the foreground
a woman stands with her baby in her arms. She is watching her husband,
as with hands tied behind his back he is being led off by a mounted trooper
who holds a gun upright before his saddle. The prisoner casts a look back,
as he is about to disappear behind a bank at the right of the composition.

Signed at the lower right, "H. Breling."

ALFRED THOMPSON BRICHER, A. N. A.

AMERICAN (1839-1908)

No. 160—   THE BROOK

PANEL

Height, 11¾ inches; width, 9¾ inches

Looking up a rocky glen, one faces a brown pool in the foreground. The
water is pouring into it by a fall, at the left of some green boulders. The
stream is seen winding between other rocks that strew the bed farther back,
until it is lost sight of in the dense growth of foliage. Conspicuous amid the
latter are two white birch stems at the right and a fir-tree high up at the left.
The foliage is dusted over with particles of light.

Signed at the lower right, "A. T. Bricher."

ROBERT SCHLEICH

GERMAN (1845-   )

No. 161—   DUTCH CANAL, WINTER

Height, 8 inches; length, 12¾ inches

ON the left bank of a frozen canal, in the foreground, a rude tent has been erected between two trees. In front of it a woman stands beside a barrel, using the top as a table from which she is dispensing some refreshment to a man in a high felt hat. A lady, handsomely attired in a fur-edged coat and salmon-pink skirt, stands beside a little girl. On the ice two men, one of them distinguished by a yellow jerkin, are in conversation, close by a little cradle-sleigh containing a child. A boy has fallen on the ice, and another boy, accompanied by a girl, skates toward him.

Signed and dated at the lower right, "ROBERT SCHLEICH, 1887, Munich."

LUIGI LOIR

AUSTRIAN

No. 162—   ENVIRONS DU PONT DE L'ARCHE

Height, 9½ inches; length, 13 inches

A GIRL, dressed in a stiff white cape and rosy-white dress, with scarlet bows in her hat, bends forward as she talks to a child. The latter wears a short drab skirt and a drab-blue waist with white collar and cuffs. The figures are standing in the center of the foreground, near some white flowers. The grass, interrupted with patches of soil, extends at the right to a row of cottages, lying beneath a smoothly beveled hill. At the left it terminates in the reedy, irregular margin of a sheet of water.

Signed at the lower right, "LOIR, LUIGI, 142."

LUIGI LOIR

AUSTRIAN

No. 163— RUE À AUBERVILLIERS

Height, 10 inches; length, 13 inches

THE spectator looks down a drab-colored street and a sidewalk of the same hue at the left of it. Here, near a lamp-post, a girl, with scarlet bows in her hair and dressed in a brownish-yellow tippet and black skirt, is walking away from the foreground. Of the same hue as the tippet are the baggy trousers of a street sweeper, working in the road. The hue also reappears in the hay with which a cart in the middle distance is piled. Meanwhile, the wheels of a *fiacre* are bright chrome, and yellow signs appear on a building and over a store at the left of the sidewalk.

Signed at the lower right, "Loir, Luigi, 182."

R. LORRAINE PYNE

No. 164— SUNSET

Height, 12 inches; width, 10 inches

A SPLENDOR of orange, yellow and rose fills the sky, bursting like a bomb above some purple woods on the horizon. A little of the glow is caught by what appears to be a small pool, low down in the middle distance. The foreground, which is enveloped in dove-gray shadow, interrupted by a little red-brown growth, slopes up to the left, where a leafless oak stands near some bushy trees.

Signed at the lower left, "Lorraine Pyne."

H. HUMPHREY MOORE

AMERICAN (1844-   )

No. 165—   THE FORTUNE TELLER

PANEL

Height, 14 inches; width, 10 inches

A SPANISH girl sits at the left of the composition, holding a guitar to the floor. With her head resting on her hand, she watches an old woman, who, squatting on the floor beside a brazier, holds three cards. The girl's pale-blue dress is swathed with a primrose shawl, embroidered in yellow, rose and blue. Another girl follows the scene with interest, as she sits sideways in the rear of the room with one arm on the back of her chair. A barrel and bottles appear on a dresser at the right.

Signed at the lower left, "H. HUMPHREY MOORE, *Paris.*"

ARTHUR HOEBER, A. N. A.

AMERICAN (1854-   )

No. 166—   EARLY MORNING

Height, 16 inches; width, 12 inches

A SANDY path winds back through the long reedy grass of the foreground. At the left a leafless tree, catching the light upon the upper part of its stem, is succeeded by a sapling, beyond which stands a trunk of sturdy growth. Where the path disappears to the right is a clump of small trees with a blur of bluish-gray foliage. The sky is astir with flusters of creamy white.

Signed at the lower left, "ARTHUR HOEBER."

LUIGI LOIR

AUSTRIAN

No. 167—   ENVIRONS DE CLAMART

Height, 10¼ inches; length, 14¼ inches

AT the right of a roadway which extends back from the foreground is an
entrance, bearing the sign "Restaurant," hung with blue and red lamps. Some
figures are entering, one of them being distinguished by a Japanese parasol.
At the left, nearer to the front, a young man has his arm around the shoulders
of a girl, while both wheel beside them their bicycles. Two women are seated
at the extreme left, their costumes presenting spots of brown and scarlet. The
road is crossed horizontally in the rear by another street, where people are seen
seated in front of a café. Wooded hills terminate the vista.

Signed at the lower right, "LOIR, LUIGI, 139."

A. BERTZIK

GERMAN

No. 168— A LADY OF THE SIXTEENTH CENTURY

Height, 15 inches; width, 11 inches

PAINTED with a precise regard for detail, the head and bust of a lady are
represented three-quarters to the right. A black velvet hat, adorned with
white and plum-colored feathers, is set at an angle on her head, revealing one
side of the blond hair, dressed with pearls. The figure is attired in a stomacher,
finishing round the neck in a gold band, a brown bodice and a mossy-green
jacket, the high standing collar and lapels of which are embellished with brown
fur. An enamel cross, set with jewels, is suspended on her breast.

Signed at the upper right, "A. BERTZIK."

JOSÉ FRAPPA

FRENCH (1854-1904)

No. 169—   THE SINGER

PANEL

Height, 17½ inches; width, 14 inches

A RED-ROBED cardinal sits at the left of the composition in front of a grand piano, his right hand fingering the keys while the left is raised. He turns a laughing face to a young abbé, whose standing figure is vested in reddish-purple biretta and cassock, while a crimson maltese cross, decorated with jewels, is suspended on his breast from a yellow and red ribbon. While he sings he holds a music book in his left hand and elevates the right, so that it seems to be pointing to a picture of St. Cecilia on the wall behind him.

Signed at the lower right, "JOSE FRAPPA."

ALFRED PERKINS

No. 170—   INCOMING TIDE

Height, 17 inches; width, 15 inches

A TRIANGLE of lavender sand, spotted with brown, shows at the right of the foreground. The gray-blue water, curdled white, is sliding toward it, followed
by long, low rolls of over-curling surf, as the waves break gently on the flat
shore. In the middle distance a lavender-brown rock projects above the water,
apparently terminating a spit of sand. Far back toward the left a schooner is
passing and a single sail appears. There is a second at the extreme right,
and others are vaguely visible on the horizon. The sky is drabbish-gray,
interrupted half way up by an interval of creamy white.

Signed at the lower right, "ALFRED PERKINS."

ANTONIO CASANOVA Y ESTORACH

SPANISH (1847-1896)

No. 171—   TASTING

Height, 18 inches; width, 15 inches

SEEN as far as the bust, a fat cardinal looks up with half-closed eyes at a
glass of champagne, which is elevated in his right hand. A bit of scarlet skull-
cap shows above his white hair and the gold spectacles which lie back upon his
forehead. A white napkin is fastened round his neck over the scarlet cassock.

Signed and dated at the upper right, "ANTONIO CASANOVA Y ESTORACH, Paris, 1892."

C. E. SWAN

BRITISH

No. 172—   LION'S HEAD

Height, 20 inches; width, 16 inches

THE head is shown three-quarters to the left against a dove-gray background. The general color of the hair and pelt is a tawny, brownish-yellow; the fringe on the chin being paler, as also the whiskers, which grow out of brown flecks. The eyes are liquid brown, the nose lavender-pink, while the rosy tongue shows between two teeth in the purplish lower jaw. The lion has a look of ferocity, though not of anger, even with the open mouth and fiercely dilated nostrils. His attention is directed keenly at something to the left and back of the spectator. Apparently it is something which he feels to be his legitimate prey, and he is ready for his meal.

Signed and dated at the lower right, "C. E. SWAN, 1900."

ANTONIO CASANOVA Y ESTORACH

SPANISH (1847-1896)

No. 173—   FRAGRANCE

Height, 18½ inches; width, 15 inches

THE bust and head of a cardinal, in scarlet cape and biretta, are seen above the corner of a mauve tablecloth. His right hand grasps a gray-blue decorated vase, containing a bunch of white, pink and crimson carnations. As he sniffs their fragrance, his lips draw back in a smile, revealing the white teeth.

Signed and dated at the upper left, "ANTONIO CASANOVA Y ESTORACH, Paris, 1893."

HENRY MOSLER, A. N. A.

AMERICAN (1841-   )

No. 174—   HAYMAKER

Height, 22 inches; width, 15½ inches

A GIRL sits facing us upon a stile, resting one elbow on a post and holding a rake to the ground. A red handkerchief is bound round her dark hair. A blue bodice, laced over a white chemisette and fastened upon the shoulders with black straps, fits over a bluish-green skirt, which is partly covered with a gray-blue apron.

Signed at the lower left, "HENRY MOSLER, Paris."

FRANK KNOX MORTON REHN, N. A.

AMERICAN (1848-   )

No. 175—   A SUMMER SEA

Height, 16 inches; length, 27 inches

Two GULLS hover over the foreground of water, where it slides toward the brown sand which spreads at the right. A little farther back the waves break gently in a series of foaming rolls, beyond which the water extends its greenish levels to a horizon, interrupted by the sails of a schooner and a small boat. They gleam white against a pale greeny-blue sky, which higher up is tenderly suffused with rose and shows at the left the sun-lit tops of some white clouds.

Signed and dated at the lower right, "F. K. M. REHN, 1875."

ARTHUR HOEBER, A. N. A.

AMERICAN (1854-   )

No. 176—   LATE AFTERNOON

Height, 14 inches; length, 22 inches

A WAVE rides across the middle distance, rearing to a point, and elsewhere toppling over and breaking into foam. The water in advance of it swirls around a glistening reef of dark-brown and reddish-yellow rocks which project from the right. The blue-green water in the foreground seethes with rosy white and cream.

Signed at the lower left, "ARTHUR HOEBER."

H. BRELING

GERMAN

No. 177—   THE SPY

PANEL

Height, 16 inches; length, 22 inches

IN front of a rude tent a soldier, in red tunic and tan boots that reach to his waist, is lifting a woman's cap from the tonsured head of a fat monk, who, dressed in female attire, kneels with hands clasped in an attitude of supplication. A little in the rear a stout woman smiles, as a man with drooping gray moustache whispers in her ear. Among the other figures which complete the scene is a young man mounted on a dapple-gray horse.

Signed at the lower left, "H. BRELING."

JULES WORMS

FRENCH (1832-   )

No. 178—   THE TOMATO SELLER

Height, 18 inches; length, 22 inches

An old man, seated in the center of a Spanish interior, turns in his chair to scrutinize the scales in which some tomatoes are being weighed by a young man, who stands at the left. Meanwhile, the latter looks over the head of his customer toward a girl, who stands by a table at the right of the background, wiping a plate. He is gaily dressed in a black beaver hat and short green jacket with scarlet sleeves, while a violet scarf is wound round the top of his olive-green breeches. The old man's costume consists of a bright yellow cap, magenta vest, a crimson sash, green breeches and white stockings.

Signed at the lower left, "J. Worms."

MADAME MARIE DIÉTERLE

FRENCH (1860-   )

No. 179—   COWS BESIDE A POOL

Height, 12½ inches; length, 16½ inches

A SEDGY pool in which some ducks are disporting themselves, occupies the right of the foreground. On the bank at the left, beneath a willow, lies a reddish-yellow cow with white face. Behind her stands a white one with a pinkish glow on her neck and shoulders. At the left is visible part of a purplish-brown cow with white face, while at the right a yellowish-red is stooping to drink. In the meadow beyond appears a man beside a white and black horse. In the distance are trees, softly silhouetted against a dove-gray horizon.

Signed at the lower left, "MARIE DIETERLE."

ANTOINE AUGUSTE ERNEST HÉBERT

FRENCH (1817-1908)

No. 180—   AN ORIENTAL BEAUTY

Height, 22 inches; width, 18 inches

THE bust, full-front, and the head, slightly to the right, of an Oriental woman are shown against a background of green leafage, flecked with yellow. Her black hair is ringed with a gold chain, from which are suspended little crescents. The eyes are immersed in brown shadow. Flat rings hang from the ears, while three strings of pearls encircle the neck. She wears a black jacket, edged and embroidered with gold, which shows the sleeves of the undergarment. These are of pinkish material, embroidered with creamy gray and barred with grayish-green. The right hand holds a dull scarlet fan.

Signed at the center right, "H."

FÉLIX ZIEM

FRENCH (1821-1911)

No. 181—   SUNSET OVER CADORE

PANEL

Height, 15 inches; length, 21¾ inches

A LINE of blue mountains, in which nestles the mountain-valley town of Pieve
de Cadore, the birthplace of Titian, extends horizontally across the distance.
Over it hangs a primrose sky, greenish above until it passes into faint blue. The
sunset is seen from across an expanse of beautiful blue water, which reaches to
the foreground. Here, at the right, a long gondola containing several figures,
one of which is in blue, while another makes a spot of geranium scarlet, is
putting out from the bank. The latter is covered with brownish and rosy grass
and occupied by a tree with a sprinkle of reddish foliage.

Signed at the lower right, "Ziem."

RENÉ BILLOTTE

FRENCH (1846-   )

No. 182—   ROUTE D'ASNIERES

Height, 18½ inches; length, 24½ inches

It is a gray day, coldly lighted, and the scene shows sharply against a dove-gray horizon, surmounted by blue. From the left of the foreground a roadway leads back, bordered at the right by a paling fence, over the top of which appear the black hat and the blue shoulders of a solitary pedestrian. At the right spreads a level of gray-green and buff grass which in the middle distance is cut into by a rectangular fenced yard, adjoining some pale-green trees. Beyond the enclosure is a horizontal row of houses, dark red in their lower stories and white above, with roofs that are colored variously drab, grayish-lavender and red. The line is continued at the left of the roadway by a house with a slate mansard roof, next to which are two conspicuously white buildings.

Signed at the lower right, "RENE BILLOTTE."

LÉON GERMAIN PELOUSE

FRENCH (1838-1891)

No. 183—   THE LOIRE AT VUILLA FAUX

Height. 18½ inches: length, 25¾ inches

THE scene is impregnated with gray; the water which flows back from the left of the foreground being a gray-blue, stained with grayish-green reflections. It passes out of sight in the middle distance at a point marked by a tall poplar which cuts against the gray-buffs and slaty-grays of a grassy hillside, while the brown, dead top of the tree shows against the sky. At the left of the poplar a cottage with reddish wall stands beside an arched bridge. Nearer to the front on the left bank appears the bright rosy-cream wall of a mill, from which a water-wheel projects over the stream.

Signed at the lower left, "L. G. PELOUSE."

.

GEORGES MICHEL

FRENCH (1763-1843)

No. 184— AN OLD OAK

Height, 24 inches; width, 19 inches

ON the left of the foreground of brownish-buff earth stands the glistening silvery trunk of an oak, which leans toward the right and spreads its torn, twisted and leafless limbs against the sky. At its foot lies another trunk, the sawn end toward the front and its splintered top reaching back to the right. Dark olive-green trees are massed in the rear and crown a knoll at the left. Above them float white clouds in a sky that grows to slaty-gray at the zenith.

W. HUGHES

BRITISH

No. 185— STILL-LIFE

PANEL

Height, 20 inches; length, 23 inches

A LARGE red-glazed earthenware crock with a lid stands on the floor in the foreground beside a bunch of celery. On a settle behind, partly covered with a white cloth, are disposed a bowl, containing lettuce, radishes and onions, an English "cottage" loaf and an oil flask, bound with straw. In the background, at the left, a door opens into a cellar, where a barrel appears.

Signed and dated at the lower right, "W. HUGHES, 1869."

ANT. MOLKENBOER

HOLLAND

No. 186—
A CITY GARDEN

Height, 24 inches; width, 18 inches

RISING from the left of the foreground, a bare tree-stem cuts the composition diagonally. A path, curving horizontally, divides the foreground from a lawn, yellow with light. It is occupied by the statue of a child, while to the left grows an elm. In the rear a well, surmounted by a cupola, adjoins a vine arbor, which extends along the façade of a red brick house. A red wall at the right, separating the garden from the street, is interrupted by a gateway, the piers of which are decorated with vases in pairs.

Signed and dated at the lower right, "ANT. MOLKENBOER, 1906."

G. FISCHER

GERMAN

No. 187—
HYACINTHS

Height, 20½ inches; length, 25½ inches

A GLASS bowl is set upon a yellow tablecloth against a pale yellow background. It contains an arrangement of blue, white and rose-colored hyacinths. Their waxy blossoms are brilliantly illumined, while the stems, seen through the glass, show softly green in the water.

Signed above the lower right, "G. FISCHER."

ARTHUR HOEBER, A. N. A.

AMERICAN (1854-   )

No. 188—   "MOON-LED WATERS WHITE"

Height, 16 inches; length, 30 inches

THE full moon hangs in a mist of faint primrose-green, and trails a path of light over the smooth, greenish-gray water and wet sand. The latter is interrupted both at the left and right of the foreground by silvery-gray and bluish rocks, rimmed upon their upper edges with rosy cream.

Signed at the lower left, "ARTHUR HOEBER."

FRANÇOIS CHARLES CACHOUD

FRENCH (CONTEMPORARY)

No. 189—   COTEAU DE ST. ALBAN

Height, 14½ inches; length, 22 inches

A BAND of water crosses the foreground, reflecting in the soft moonlight tones of blue, dove-gray and olive. The opposite bank is fringed with bulrushes and tawny yellow reeds and grass. At the right, in the middle distance, three gray, olive-green poplars rise like spectres out of a mass of blurred pale-green and darker green foliage. At the left an irregular row of six cottages, with brown-red roofs and walls, greenish-primrose in the moonlight, shows against a clump of purplish trees and an olive-brown smoothly beveled hill. Three stars prick the greeny-gray blue of the sky, while at the zenith hover two fleecy olive-gray clouds.

Signed and dated at the lower right, "F. CACHOUD, 1906."

G. A. TRAVER

No. 190—   LANDSCAPE

Height, 24 inches; width, 18 inches

Two TREES grow close together in the extreme left of the foreground. Their stems are seen against a brownish mottle of foliage. This belongs to some smaller trees on the farther bank of a stream which curves round to the right of the foreground. It reflects the butter-colored glow of the horizon, which is also tinged with cool green tones in the shadow under the bank. From the latter the meadow extends back to a clump of trees at the right. In the distance at the left lies a dove-gray hill. The sky over the horizon is yellow, curdled with cream, passing thence to a green that gradually grows bluer.

Signed at the lower left, "G. A. TRAVER."

ANTONIO TORREZ

SPANISH

No. 191—   A SPANISH BEAUTY

Height, 24 inches; width, 18½ inches

WHILE the lady's head is posed three-quarters to the right, the bust is inclined in the opposite direction. The type is characteristically Spanish; crimson lips, hazel eyes and darkened eyebrows. The black, curled hair is adorned with fluffy pompons of deep rose silk, over which is draped a white mantilla. The latter hangs down to the right shoulder and is drawn over the left arm, leaving visible only a little of the yellow bodice.

Signed at the lower left, "ANTONIO TORREZ."

GUILLAUME R. FOUACE

FRENCH (-1895)

No. 192—   CHICKEN AND HAM

Height, 20 inches; length, 26 inches

A ROAST fowl, browned over in parts, is laid on a plate with its feet doubled back over the breast. The head has not been removed, and a sharp-pointed, silver-handled knife lies across the neck. The dish is decorated with a small running pattern of red volutes and blue and green leaves. At the back, toward the left, appears the shank half of a boiled ham, while to the right stands a green glass jar with the cork half drawn.

Signed at the lower right, "G. FOUACE."

A. VOIGT

GERMAN

No. 193—   COWS IN PASTURE

Height, 18 inches; length, 25½ inches

THE yellow-green herbage, sprinkled with white and lavender flowers and some scarlet poppies, extends back to a horizontal strip of yellow stubble, with two wheat-ricks at the extreme right. A level sweep of lavender hill completes the vista, showing faintly against a drab sky, sifted over with dove-colored vapor. It is broken into at the left by a buff glare from which distant rain is falling. Near the center of the foreground a red and white cow lies with her head away from the spectator. At her left stands a brownish-red, splashed with white, while farther back at the right a drab cow lies, facing the front, and a yellow one, seen in profile, is grazing.

Signed at the lower right, "A. VOIGT."

JULIAN RIX

AMERICAN (1851-1903)

No. 194—   STUDY OF A SNOW SCENE

Height, 24 inches; width, 16 inches

A FEW spiky dead stems prick the snowy foreground, while at the right rises a knoll, surmounted by two slender tree trunks. At the left of the foreground a lamp-post, painted blue, stands beside two young cypresses. Near the center of the middle distance a group of drab and slaty sheds appears behind a tree, whose straggly limbs grow out from near the ground. The suggestion of other trees in the rear is faintly indicated.

Signed at the lower right, "JULIAN RIX."

ARTHUR HOEBER, A. N. A.

AMERICAN (1854-   )

No. 195—   HYANNIS PORT MARSHES

Height, 20 inches; length 30 inches

THE foreground is covered with a tangle of rich green switchy grass, sprinkled with yellow iris. In the middle distance the greenish-gray water serpentines through the yellow-green marshes, which, as they recede, become green, and at the right pass into blue. The horizon is thick with dove-gray vapor above which emerge volumes of rosy lavender-creamy cloud, silhouetted against the sky's pale gray-blue.

Signed at the lower left, "ARTHUR HOEBER."

CLAUS MEYER

GERMAN (1856-   )

No. 196—   THE LETTER

Height, 25½ inches; width, 20½ inches

THE picture, painted in imitation of Vermeer of Delft, represents a young lady standing in profile before a table at the left, reading a letter. With the exception of a curl which strays over the cheek, the hair is drawn back and dressed on the crown. The latter cuts into a landscape picture, showing a white horse, which hangs on the wall. The girl is dressed in an olive-green skirt and a jacket of rosy-purple velvet, edged with white fur. Among the articles on the table lies an envelope with a red seal. A tapestry curtain is draped down the left of the composition.

Signed and dated at the upper right, "CLAUS MEYER, Munich, '90."

JEAN GUSTAVE JACQUET

FRENCH (1846-1909)

No. 197— TÊTE CITOYENNE

Height, 24 inches; width, 20 inches

THE figure, shown as far as the waist, three-quarters to the right, is attired in an Empire gown of silvery-pink satin, fastened at the waist with a golden amber sash and bordered round the low bosom with the two flounces of a soft fichu. The lady's golden chestnut hair, fringed over the forehead, dressed in a roll upon the crown and bound with an apple-green ribbon, is set off with a pink ostrich plume. Her hazel eyes are fixed on the spectator. She wears a black velvet band round the neck, and earrings which are composed of a diamond, emerald and gold drop.

Signed at the lower left, "G. JACQUET."

LÉON RICHET

FRENCH (1847-1907)

No. 198—   LANDSCAPE WITH FIGURE

PANEL

Height, 19 inches; length, 27¼ inches

THE olive-green herbage of the foreground is interrupted by little pockets of water, reflecting gray or cream light, by one or two boulders and by tussets of coarse brown grass. Some distance back, at the right, a woman in a crimson skirt, blackish body and white cap, is bending beneath the weight of a faggot held in front of her. She is approaching a white-walled cottage with golden-red and olive roof, which occupies a shady knoll, overhung with trees. In the middle distance, at the left, appear a bright crimson roof and white chimney. The center distance shows a vista of meadow, barred by yellow iight. It leads back to where rosy-red roofs nestle under yellow trees.

Signed and dated at the lower left, "LEON RICHET, '72."

ALEXANDRE NOZAL

FRENCH

No. 199—   SPRING LANDSCAPE

Height, 20 inches; length, 26 inches

DIAGONALLY across the right of the foreground runs a path, bordered with grass and a sprinkle of violet and yellow flowers. It passes a fragment of fence, attached to the trunk of a sycamore, fledged with young leaves. Behind it small peach trees with faint, rosy blossoms grow out of a hedge that crosses to the left. Here an apple tree with a mass of white blossom rises beside a strip of tall wheat. More trees show beyond, and over their tops appear the red roofs of houses and of the nave of a church with a spire. The vista terminates in a gray-lavender hill.

Signed and dated at the lower left, "A. NOZAL, Gareches, (S.O.)"

LÉON GERMAIN PELOUSE

FRENCH (1838-1891)

No. 200—   NEAR BOURG-PRÈS-MORTAIN

Height, 18 inches; length, 26 inches

TWILIGHT is settling over the village street, which leads directly to the foreground. A woman, in white cap, dark brown body and blue apron, approaches c a r r y i n g a basket. Farther back at the left, two women converse near a well, the slaty-blue hood of which shows against the bright green thatch of a high-pitched roof. On the opposite side of the road a bay horse in a cart stands beside a house which has dormer-windows projecting from its slate roof. The distance is closed in with drab trees, showing faintly against the cold, pale cream of the horizon, over which lies a bar of grayish-claret cloud.

Signed at the lower right, "L. G. PELOUSE."

FERNAND EMMANUEL PELEZ

FRENCH (1843-   )

No. 201—   THE BAKER'S BOY

Height, 29½ inches; width, 16 inches

WITH a smile on his large mouth, a boy stands facing the spectator, both hands raised to steady a basket on his head, containing a pie. A baker's white linen cap partly covers his blond hair, which is shaved close, giving extra prominence to his projecting ears. He wears a double-breasted white coat and a white apron over short, olive-drab trousers. The figure is seen against brown paneled woodwork.

Signed at the lower left, "F. PELEZ."

ARTHUR HOEBER, A. N. A.

AMERICAN (1854-   )

No. 202—   THE COAL WHARF

Height, 20 inches; length, 30 inches

A WHARF projects horizontally from the left of the middle distance, lined with
various craft. A white sail glistens in the moonlight behind the gray-green
hull of a steamboat whose greenish-blue funnel is marked with red. Off the end
of the wharf lies a sailboat with dark blue hull. At the right of it in the
greening sky a ring of rosy-cream vapor surrounds a misty full moon.

Signed at the lower right, "ARTHUR HOEBER."

JULIAN RIX

AMERICAN (1851-1903)

No. 203—   STILL LIFE

PANEL

Height, 20 inches; length, 32½ inches

VARIOUS articles of masculine contentment are disposed in a brown, shadowed
niche in a silvery-drab wall. A cigar, which shows a rim of red beneath the
ash, projects over the edge of the masonry. Behind it is an open packet
from which some flakes of tobacco have escaped. They lie beside the well-
colored bowl of a clay pipe, the stem of which rests against the ringed handle
of a schnapps flask. At the left of the latter stands a benedictine bottle.

Signed at the lower right, "JULIAN RIX."

P. MARCOTTE DE QUIVIÈRES

FRENCH (CONTEMPORARY)

No. 204—   THE FISHING FLEET

Height, 20 inches; length, 29 inches

THE drab and brownish-red sails of the fishing fleet spot the middle distance
and stretch to the horizon, where a streak of light, or it may be shore, separates
the water from a sky, turbulent with slaty-purple vapor.   In the foreground
the gray water is sliding over the flat sand, its ripples frilled with white and
showing pale green in their hollows.   Some small rocks, covered with bright
green seaweed, appear at the right, while two gulls are flying low over the
water at the left.

Signed at the lower left, "P. MARCOTTE DE QUIVIERES."

LOUIS NEUBERT

GERMAN (1846-1892)

No. 205—   NEAR MARSEILLES

Height, 16 inches; length, 31½ inches

FROM the left of the foreground, marked by two small rocks, the pinkish-drab
sand extends to the right.   It is sprinkled with stones and terminates in a
distant spit, where figures are visible beside a boat.   The beach is bounded
in the rear by a sea-wall, over the center of which appears a building, composed of a series of rectangular masses, crowned with a tower.   At the left is a
cypress, beyond which spreads a hillside, dotted with houses and surmounted by
a row of cypresses that show dark against the primrose of the sky.

Signed at the lower left, "L. NEUBERT."

LÉON RICHET

FRENCH (1847-1907)

No. 206—   L'ALMÉE

PANEL

Height, 29 inches; width, 23¾ inches

An Oriental lady is seated at the right of a shady garden retreat, watching
languidly a dancing girl. The latter, while she holds a veil behind her body
with extended hands, sways to the left, her brown hair floating loosely from a
crimson cap decorated with sequins. Her costume consists of a white under-
skirt and an upper one of old rose, which is fastened round the waist with a
gold band and embellished with a sash. Close behind her kneels a girl in a
green drapery, waving aloft a tambourine. Two other girls are seated in front,
at the left, with their backs toward the spectator. A mandolin lies beside one
of them and in the center of the foreground stands a low tabouret, holding a
flask and three liqueur glasses.

Signed and dated at the lower right, "LEON RICHET, 1881."

ARTHUR HOEBER, A. N. A.

AMERICAN (1854-   )

No. 207—   CAPE MARSHES

Height, 20 inches; length, 30 inches

THE level vista, clothed with coarse, juicy herbage, passes back in tones of
green that yield to cream, which in turn changes to yellow and thence to a
bluish and yellowish-green at the horizon. Over the latter float layers of
creamy cloud, tinged toward the zenith with rose. The sky's hues are caught
in a flare of reflection on the surface of a pool in the foreground, fringed with
reeds.

Signed at the lower left, "ARTHUR HOEBER."

HEINRICH FUNK

GERMAN (1807-1877)

No. 208—   LANDSCAPE

Height, 19 inches; length, 31 inches

A LARGE oak occupies the center of the foreground, gripping the bank with its roots. At the right of it two women, one having her arm round the other's waist, are mounting a pathway which ascends and then curves round to an eminence that appears at the left of the oak. Here two figures are worshipping before a little shrine, surmounted by a cross.

Signed at the lower right, "H. FUNK."

C. AYER WHIPPLE

AMERICAN

No. 209—   STRAY NOTES

Height, 30 inches; width 18 inches

STANDING back to the spectator in front of a piano, with her left knee resting on a chair so that the sole of her shoe is exposed, a lady looks down at a sheet of music, while her right hand strays over the keys. A rosy-white gauze fichu, revealing her right shoulder and neck, envelopes the body of her gown, which is of dull scarlet material, silvered over with lavender and bluish tones. Her head shows against an etching that hangs on the opposite wall.

Signed and dated at the lower right, "C. AYER WHIPPLE, 1901."

RENÉ BILLOTTE

No. 210—   ROUTE DE LA RÉVOLTE   . .

Height, 21¼ inches; length, 31½ inches

FROM the foreground recedes a vista of broad footpath, bordered with leafless trees at the left, where it is paralleled by the roadway and the opposite footpath. On the last a solitary figure is passing a fence and advertising board, beyond which stand a white and a drab house, both showing red frames to the doorways. A wagon with a load of straw breaks the monotony of the roadway, while on the footpath at the right appear two figures in the middle distance and in the foreground a group of three children, following a woman dressed in white. Vacant lots extend along the right of the footpath.

Signed at the lower left, "RENE BILLOTTE."

FRANÇOIS FLAMENG

FRENCH (1856-   )

No. 211—   WITH BONAPARTE IN ITALY

Height, 25 inches; length 39½ inches

THE scene commemorates Bonaparte's famous campaign against the Austrians in Northern Italy, 1796-97. The army, fresh from its victories at Castiglione, Rivoli and Roverbello, is on the march to Verona. Bonaparte, accompanied by his staff, rides across the foreground toward the right. Distinguished by a tricolor sash, he occupies the right of the front rank, the officers at his left being General Berthier, Chief of Staff, and General La Harpe, commanding the First Division. The personages in the second file, reckoning from the left, are General Masséna, commander of the Second Division; Lannes, Colonel of Hussars, and Eugène Beauharnais, Bonaparte's adopted son, serving as his aide-de-camp. Behind the last named rides Marot, Colonel of Chasseurs, at whose side, conspicuous by his long hair, is Auguereau, now commanding the Third Division and later to be made Duke of Castiglione. The staff is escorted by a troop of Hussars, while on the lower ground in the distance at the left regiments appear, extended in line formation and crossing a pontoon bridge. In the middle distance at the right lies the little town of Roverbello, its towers rising against purple mountains, above which soar the snowy peaks of the Italian Alps.

Signed at the lower right, "FRANÇOIS FLAMENG."

JEAN LÉON GÉRÔME

FRENCH (1824-1904)

No. 212— THE TULIP CRAZE

Height, 26¼ inches; length, 39½ inches

On a pathway adjoining a vista of rectangular patches of tulips, scarlet, pink, purple and other hues, a dandy of the seventeenth century stands pointing his rapier down to a pot containing a rose-colored blossom. He is fantastically attired in a drab felt cylindrical hat, adorned with a black plume; white ruff; a brown doublet with blue silk sleeves; trunks of a lighter brown and a black velvet cloak. In response to his gesture, two soldiers in steel morions and breastplates, leather jerkins and boots that reach to the thighs, are hurrying forward on the run. Meanwhile, the rest of the company, in charge of a mounted officer, are heedlessly trampling over the tulip beds in the rear. The scene is bounded by a row of houses with dull red roofs, over the top of which rises a high narrow tower, surmounted by a lantern spire.

Tulips were introduced into Europe by the Turks. In 1559 one Conrad Gesner brought them from Turkey to Augsburg. Thence they were imported into Holland, Haarlem becoming, as it still remains, the center of the industry. During the seventeenth century occurred "the tulip craze," when speculation carried the price of bulbs in certain instances up to 2,500 florins, and even, according to some writers, as high as 4,600 florins.

Signed at the right of the lower center, "J. L. GÉRÔME."

FREDERICK AUGUST VON KAULBACH

GERMAN (1850-   )

No. 213—   DAY DREAMS

Height, 39½ inches; width, 29½ inches

A GARDEN bench, painted red, is disposed across the foreground.   At the right
end of it a lady sits with her left leg crossed over the knee of the other, seen
in profile, while her body and face are turned to the front, the gray eyes being
fixed on the spectator.   Her right arm extends along the top of the bench,
the hand holding a book, while the other hand lies upon her lap.   Her dark
hair is decked with a tortoise-shell comb, the head being silhouetted against a
mass of pale gray-green foliage.   She wears a white dress of soft material
that reflects tones of cream, lavender-pink and very pale red-plum.   Black
velvet bands encircle the shoulders and cross the bosom, and a sash of dark gray
silk confines the waist.   A bush of pink and white camelias grows at the left
of the foreground.

Signed on the top of the bench, "F. A. KAULBACH."

WERNER SCHUCH

GERMAN (1843-   )

No. 214—   THE BATTLE OF LEIPZIG

Height, 34 inches; length, 43½ inches

THE picture commemorates the victory of the Prussians and their Russian, Austrian and Swedish allies over Napoleon, October 16-19, 1813. General Schwarzenberg is shown, surrounded by his staff. The group occupies a summit at the right, overlooking the battle which is proceeding down below in the distance at the left. An aide-de-camp, dressed in a gray frock coat with red collar and gray, tightly buttoned breeches, is reporting something to the General, who wears an olive-green coat and cocked hat with a white feather. Between the two is a third figure, wearing a pale blue coat with high red collar and a green feather in his gold-trimmed hat. At the immediate right of the foreground two officers, one of them notably stout, are on foot, studying a map.

Signed at the lower right, "WERNER SCHUCH."

FRITZ VON UHDE

GERMAN (1848-1911)

No. 215—   THE FLIGHT

Height, 48¼ inches; width, 39½ inches.

THIS is one of the artist's pictures of the Bible story translated into the ver-
nacular, as it were, of Bavarian peasant life. The young mother sits leaning
against a trunk at the right of a grove of yellow beech trees. Her feet are
stretched out; one hand rests in her lap; the other hangs to the ground; the
gesture of the whole body being eloquent of weariness. Her baby is on the
lap of a gray-haired, gray-bearded man who sits facing the spectator, almost
completely enveloped in a brown cloak. The donkey is seen, grazing behind
the trees at the right, where the pasture is flooded with yellow light. In the
foreground at the left lies a carpenter's bag, filled with tools.

Signed at the lower right, "VON UHDE."

PINKNEY MARCIUS-SIMONS

AMERICAN (1867-1909)

No. 216— SUNDAY MORNING, MAISON LAFITTE

Height, 21 inches; length, 36 inches

A BUILDING occupies the back of a little court, shaded by trees and enlivened with figures. From a doorway at the left of the façade, surmounted by a statue of Madonna and Child, lit by soft sunshine, some girls are appearing, headed by one in a scarlet cloak and another in pale blue body and pink skirt. In the middle distance a young man stands reading a newspaper, while a companion, leaning against a tree, looks over his shoulder. At the left of the foreground an old man, seated with his back to the spectator, turns his head to listen to a friend at his side who is gesticulating as he talks. At the extreme right a young girl in black hood and cloak, carrying a prayer-book, walks beside a child.

Signed at the lower right, "MARCIUS-SIMONS."

ALBERT LOREY GROLL, A. N. A.

AMERICAN (1866-   )

No. 217—   RIDGEFIELD, NEW JERSEY

Height, 25 inches; length, 35 inches

THE foreground of meadow, broken up with tones of yellow, green and russet, slopes up at the right to a knoll, crowned with maples. Their foliage, where it shows against the sky, flares scarlet, while the central mass is green, passing into red and golden yellow. A little distance back from the left of the foreground grow a few crimson flowers, beyond which the ground rises, creamy yellow, to a clump of orange-tawny trees. To the right of them appear some buildings, particularly the end of a house with a gambrel roof, which catch the light. They are seen against a distant level range of grayish-green hill. The sky, creamy over the horizon, is tinged above with pale green that changes toward the zenith into bluish purple.

Signed at the lower right, "A. L. GROLL."

ARTHUR HOEBER, A. N. A.

AMERICAN (1854-   )

No. 218—   SUMMER EVENING

Height, 22 inches; length. 30 inches

OVER the flat sand the gray water, flecked with blue, slides in advance of two long, low sweeps of curling wave. The horizon is blurred with lavender mist, above which are dimples of rosy cream and a full moon, enveloped in creamy vapor.

Signed and dated at the lower left, "ARTHUR HOEBER, 1907."

JULIAN RIX

AMERICAN (1851-1903)

No. 219—   PASSAIC VALLEY

Height, 34½ inches; width, 21½ inches

IN the fitful light from a blue sky, scattered with tufts and volumes of white and gray vapor, a patch of grass near the foreground shows yellow-green. It is intersected by a path, which curves back to a gray-green shed, attached to another at right angles. The light also yellows the foliage of a big tree and some smaller ones which crown a gentle slope at the right. Beyond the illuminated foreground a wooded valley, deep blue in shadow, save for touches of red roofs and some flecks of light, extends back to distant, wooded hills, whose purple hue is interrupted by pale lavender and dove-gray.

Signed and dated at the lower right, "JULIAN RIX, '98."

E. KEYSER

GERMAN

No. 220— BRINGING HOME THE APPLE BOUGH

Height, 26 inches; length, 33¾ inches

THREE children are coming down a gentle incline, descending from the right, where a bunch of willows stand. The foremost of the group, a little girl in a white cap with faint rose and cream kerchief over her gray-lavender bodice, is carrying a bough of apple blossoms. It is also supported by an older girl, with soft chestnut-brown hair, braided at the neck, who is dressed in an old rose bodice and olive-black skirt. She holds the hand of a small child, who grasps the girl's arm with her other hand and lays her face against it.

Signed at the lower left, "E KEYSER."

CESARE DETTI

ITALIAN (1848-   )

No. 221— THE STANDARD BEARER

Height, 36½ inches; width, 29 inches

A FLAG, with indications of rose and buff devices, on a mossy-green ground, is held over the left shoulder of a man whose figure is shown as far as the hips, three-quarters to the right. The brim of a round black hat encircles his brown hair, which is arranged in curls over the ears. His moustache, turned up at the ends, is light chestnut. A soft white collar, edged with lace, falls over his cream and gold silk damask vest, which is fastened by a close row of buttons and embellished at the waist with silvery bluish-green tags. Over this is worn a rich mantle of pearly silk with a salmon-rose turnover collar. A glimpse of lining of the same color shows at the wrist of the man's right hand, which is planted on the hip.

Signed at the upper right, "C. DETTI."

GASTON DE LATENAY

FRENCH

No. 222—   NEAR BORDEAUX

Height, 32 inches; length, 44 inches

THE sea spreads a smooth green surface, tinged with tones of sapphire in the
ripples of the foreground.   A few little puffs of dove-gray vapor float in the
lower part of the gray-blue sky.   Near the front, at the right, is a French
fishing-smack with two creamy sails and one blackish-red.   Over at the left are
two other boats, distinguished, respectively, by the red and the blue of their
hulls.   In the central distance appears a packet-steamer with red funnel.

Signed at the lower right, "G. LATENAY."

LÉON GERMAIN PELOUSE

FRENCH (1838-1891)

No. 223—   STUDY OF TREES

Height, 43½ inches; width, 31½ inches

A LITTLE knoll on the coast is occupied by three scraggy trees, driven over
and wrenched into tortuous shape by wind.   Their upper limbs are tufted with
foliage, while the greenish-black trunks, apparently overgrown with ivy, show
dark against a farther mass of soft, silvery, brownish-gray leafage.   A strip
of lavender-pink sea appears at the left, beneath a gray sky, curdled with
cream, that passes above to dove-pink and at the zenith to pale blue.   At the
right of the trees a peasant woman, in white winged cap, olive-slaty skirt and
rough drab apron, stands leaning over a little child who is seated on the
ground.

Signed at the lower left, "L. G. PELOUSE."

THOMAS CRESWICK

BRITISH (1811-1869)

No. 224—   A MOORLAND STREAM

Height, 34½ inches; length, 44½ inches

THE scene is a rocky glen, running up into the side of a moor, the summit of which shows in the extreme background against the blue and white sky. The foreground presents a picturesque confusion of boulders which form irregular banks to a stream. The latter in the middle distance spreads to an olive-brown golden pool, whence it descends in two falls and brawls among the stones in the foreground. A fisherman is casting a fly over the pool, while his companion stoops toward the water. Behind them grows a cluster of young beech trees, with autumn foliage of golden reddish hue.

PAUL WAGNER

GERMAN

No. 225—   CHILDREN FISHING

Height, 35½ inches; length, 51½ inches

FROM some reeds at the left a boat projects diagonally across the foreground. A girl is seated in the stern, scraping a fish before putting it into a tub at the bottom of the boat. She is dressed in a straw hat, a bodice of green, pink, drab and slaty plaid, a grayish-blue apron and a brown skirt. A little child holds her arm with one hand, while the other grasps a fish. In the bow a boy, whose trousers are turned up over bare legs and feet, stands fishing with a stick for a rod. Beside him are two smaller children, one holding a piece of bread and butter and pointing at the float, the other gazing into the water. The group is seen against a pleasant background of greenish-yellow hillside, sprinkled with trees.

Signed at the lower left, "PAUL WAGNER, München."

JEAN BAPTISTE ROBIE

FLEMISH (1821-1899)

No. 226—   ROSES

PANEL

Height, 51½ inches; width, 37½ inches

THE center of the mass is occupied by a magnificent profusion of *Gloire de Dijon* roses, buds and full-blown flowers, the latter showing pinkish-yellow in their hearts. At the lower right is a cluster of bluish-red and silvery roses, possibly *La France*, surmounted by some blossoms of deep crimson hue. A few of the latter variety are also sprinkled at the lower left.

Signed at the lower right, "J. ROBIE."

FÉLIX ZIEM

FRENCH (1821-1911)

No. 227—   INUNDATION, PLACE ST. MARC

Height, 51½ inches; width, 38¾ inches.

THE foreground presents a sheet of richly colored water. It is bounded at the right by the three flagstaffs, with red and yellow gonfalons, and at the left by the portal of St. Mark's. Gondolas are moored in front of it. The water extends to the column of St. Mark, beyond which appears, lit with rosy glow, the Campanile of San Giorgio Maggiore.

Purchased by the late owner from E. CRONIER, Paris, previous to his public sale, 1905.
Signed at the lower left, "ZIEM."

FRITZ VON LENBACH

GERMAN (1836-1904)

No. 228—   PORTRAIT OF BISMARK

Height, 51 inches; width, 39½ inches.

"THE IRON CHANCELLOR" is shown three-quarters length, about full-front, the head inclined three-quarters to the left. The top of the head is bald; the hair over the ears being, like the moustache, gray-blond. The left hand holds the hilt of the sword, while the right rests on a green-covered table. The figure is encased in a double-breasted black frock coat, with yellow collar and epaulets of twisted gold thread, while a narrow yellow stripe surrounds the cuffs. The Iron Cross is fastened over the left breast.

Signed above the lower left, "F. LENBACH."

C. AYER WHIPPLE

AMERICAN

No. 229—PORTRAIT OF JOHN HAY, THE LATE SECRETARY OF STATE

Height, 52 inches; width, 40 inches.

THE Secretary, in characteristic, alert and affable, though serious, expression, is shown at three-quarter length, seated erect in a high-backed armchair upholstered in reddish-brown leather, his face and gaze turned slightly to the right. He wears a black business suit and a dark cravat with a pearl pin. In his right hand is a gray-olive bound book, closed, but with a finger between the pages; the left hand falls easily over the opposite arm of the chair. His knees are crossed and the painter has rendered the whole pose as one of dignified ease. The head and face have been carefully worked up for likeness and lifelike expression. The light falls upon the sitter from his right, the high light of the portrait being on the right brow.

Signed at the left, C. AYER WHIPPLE, 1906.

THIRD EVENING'S SALE

WEDNESDAY, JANUARY 17TH, 1912

IN THE GRAND BALL ROOM OF THE PLAZA

FIFTH AVENUE, 58TH TO 59TH STREETS

BEGINNING AT 8 O'CLOCK

LUIGI LOIR

AUSTRIAN

No. 230—   A PARIS QUAY—EVENING

PANEL

Height, 6 inches; length, 8½ inches

THE pavement of the quay, lavender rosy-buff in color, extends straight back from the left of the foreground. It is enlivened with figures, some of which are gathered round a dull-red square ticket office, while a man dressed in black and wearing a high hat is walking toward the iron gangway that connects with the pontoon which carries the steamboat waiting-station. In the rear appear two flat arches of a bridge, one of which is cut by the smoke of a tug. A pale primrose light suffuses the evening sky.

Signed at the lower left, "LOIR, LUIGI."

H. BRELING

GERMAN

No. 231—   THE DRINKER

PANEL

Height, 6¾ inches; width, 4½ inches

A MAN, three-quarters to the spectator, is seated astride a chair, resting his elbow on the back and holding his chin in his hand. The left hand grasps a long glass of red wine as it rests on his leg. His costume includes a felt hat, set off with a stiff brown feather, a creamy white jacket, olive-brown breeches and dull rose-red stockings. A flagon stands on the floor at the left.

Signed at the upper left, "H. BRELING."

LUIGI LOIR

AUSTRIAN

No. 232— PLAGE À ST. CAST

Height, 10 inches; length, 14 inches

FROM the foreground the vista of esplanade extends back to a building with
red brick and white plaster walls and slate roofs, surmounted by a tower.
Beyond the mass lies a horizontal range of wooded hill.   The walk is enlivened
with figures, conspicuous among which are a lady in a dark tippet and brown
dress; another in a drab costume and a third who, as she sits on a bench,
displays part of her white petticoat under a black gown, dotted with white.
The sand at the left forms a curve round the gray water, against which the
white caps and aprons of three *bonnes* in charge of some children strike distinct
notes.

Signed at the lower right, "LOIR, LUIGI, 116."

PINCKNEY MARCIUS SIMONS

AMERICAN (1867-1909)

No. 233— GATHERING SHADOWS

PANEL

Height, 9½ inches; length, 14½ inches

THE sky presents   a ferment of slaty clouds, growing grayer at the right,
where peaks of rosy lavender emerge from a bank of pinkish, slaty vapor.
Rosy light illumines a pile of architecture on the summit of a knoll.   In the
middle distance, at the left, a dark figure, hooded and cloaked, walks beside a
woman whose cap and waist are white.   Nearer to the front, in the center of
the composition, are two trees, whose branches, covered with bushy brown
foliage, grow from near the ground.   A signboard at the right announces
"Chasse Gardée."   In the foreground, a woman with a bundle on her head
stands near another who kneels beside a pool, beating her linen with a mallet.

Signed at the lower right, "MARCIUS-SIMONS."

MAX SCHÖDL

GERMAN (1834-   )

No. 234—   OBJETS DE VERTU

Height, 13½ inches; width, 9½ inches

A DEEP blue silk drapery, embroidered with roses and leaves, hangs at the left of the foreground, over the edge of a table. On the latter are disposed various *objets de vertu*. In front of a cabinet, whose panels are embellished with white flowers, stands a jar, mounted on three legs, with a kylin on the lid. The body is decorated with a blue and red design in which is a panel representing a garden scene. At the right stands an ivory image, toned to brown in parts, of a woman with draped head, dressed in a kimono, who holds a rosary in one hand and in the other a long basket containing two lotus blossoms. By her side stands a child, whose hand is raised with the palm toward the spectator.

Signed and dated at the upper right, "MAX SCHODL, 1889."

JEAN RICHARD GOUBIE

FRENCH (1842-   )

No. 235—   EN CHASSE

Height, 11½ inches; length, 15 inches

A LADY, in black habit, high hat and white gloves, rides with easy seat a dark brown horse, which is approaching at a walk in the center of the foreground. She has gained the summit of a slope and turns her head to the left, as if speaking to a huntsman in pink coat and blue breeches, whose chestnut horse has all but reached the top. The head and shoulders of another huntsman, his horse's head and the head of a gentleman in a high hat are emerging from below. The foreground at the left shows slabs of rock, while elsewhere its yellowish grass is sprinkled with brown scrub. Birch woods close the scene.

Signed and dated at the lower left, "RICHARD GOUBIE, 1892."

ANTONIO CASANOVA Y ESTORACH

SPANISH (1847-1896)

No. 236— FLIRTATION

Height, 16 inches; width, 13 inches

A FAT brother of the Carthusian order, in creamy-white hood and habit, is seated beside a Spanish beauty at an open window. As he rests his chin between his thumb and forefinger and ogles her with a leer, the lady holds her fan between his face and hers. Her black hair is dressed with a tortoise-shell comb, from which a white lace mantilla falls over the shoulders of her pink-and-green damask silk bodice.

Signed and dated at the lower center, "ANTONIO CASANOVA Y ESTORACH, Paris, 1882."

LOUIS NEUBERT

GERMAN (1846-1892)

No. 237—

NEAR MARSEILLES

PANEL

Height, 7¾ inches; length, 15½ inches

THE tide is out and the flat wet sand, interrupted with little pools and masses of yellow-brown seaweed, reflects the hues of the creamy sky and the dove-gray clouds, rimmed with primrose, which hover over the horizon. From the foreground at the right a boy, carrying a basket, is walking toward some figures in the middle distance. Here beside a barrow a man in blue apron is raking, and a woman waits near him, dressed in a white cap and brown shawl. Farther back on this side a shepherd and his flock are visible on a yellow slope. Near the foreground at the left three figures are stooping beside the edge of the water.

Signed at the lower right, "L. NEUBERT."

LUIGI LOIR

AUSTRIAN

No. 238—

BOIS DE BOULOGNE

Height, 16¼ inches; width, 13 inches

SNOW covers the ground, the branches of the trees and roofs of several buildings. It is tinged with blue from the light of the electric lamps, which glow softly in the misty lavender atmosphere. At the right of the foreground a man, dressed like the footman of a private motor-car, stands behind a fence. He appears to be in attendance on a lady who is seated in front of the fence, while a boy puts on her skates She is dressed in an olive-brown skirt and a black jacket, trimmed with brown fur. At the left of the boy two advertising boards are propped against a post. The scene at the back is animated with groups of figures.

Signed at the lower left, "LOIR, LUIGI."

OSCAR LOUIS ÉDOUARD MASCRE

FRENCH

No. 239—   FLOWERING FIELDS

Height, 11½ inches; length, 15½ inches

THE foreground of yellowish-green grass is profusely spotted with yellow
daisies, interspersed with a few red poppies. It passes in the middle distance
to smooth green, which at the right is replaced by lavender-pink and blue. A
church-spire shows above the lavender-brown roofs of a group of cottages that
lie at the foot of a wooded slope. In the extreme distance, at the right, looms
the lavender and violet mass of a high hill, whose craggy summit rises to a
small peak.

Signed at the lower right, "O. MASCRE."

CLAUS MEYER

GERMAN (1856-   )

No. 240—   THE STUDENT

Height, 15¾ inches; width, 13¾ inches

SEATED at a table, with his back three-quarters to the spectator, a young man,
of studious and refined expression, turns his face over his left shoulder toward
the front. His figure is shown only to the level of the table-top, on which
the left arm is extended, the hand grasping a tall glass, decorated with three
rings and a colored device. His right hand holds a clay pipe in the mouth.
The round brim of a black hat encircles the brown hair, which is worn long to
the shoulders. A broad white collar, cut square at the back, lies flat upon a
scarlet tunic, which has cuffs at the elbows, revealing the full white sleeves of
the shirt.

Signed and dated at the upper left, "CLAUS MEYER, '86."

PIERRE EMMANUEL DAMOYE

FRENCH (1847-   )

No. 245—   LANDSCAPE

PANEL

Height, 12¾ inches; length, 23½ inches

THE foreground is filled with marshy water which reflects the faint blue of
the sky in tones of gray. Its surface is interrupted by spiky reeds, pale
yellow growth and a sprinkle of white flowers.   Some distance back, at the left,
a duck is swimming, while in the same plane at the right appear the reflections
of four branchless trunks that grow on the farther bank.   They are interspersed with three trees, crowned, respectively, with yellow, green and yellowish-
brown foliage. .In the middle distance, at the left, the seated figure of a woman
in a white hat is seen against a strip of creamy green.

Signed and dated at the lower left, "E. DAMOYE, '88."

ÉDOUARD ROSSET-GRANGER

FRENCH (1853-   )

No. 246—   THE JEWEL CASE

Height, 18 inches; length, 21 inches

A YOUNG lady, seen as far as the waist, sits looking down at a pearl necklace, of
which she holds the ends with extended hands, as it lies across an open jewel
box.   The latter rests upon a table at her right, which also supports an electric
light standard, fitted with a yellow shade.   Meanwhile, a rosy glow comes from
the right and illumines one side of her face and touches here and there the
lavender-pink of her teagown, which is embellished with lace at the neck
and sleeves.

Signed at the lower left, "E. ROSSET-GRANGER."

GABRIEL CORNELIS VON MAX

AUSTRIAN (1840-   )

No. 247—   SUSANNE

Height, 19 inches; width, 15½ inches

FACING three-quarters to the right are shown the head and bust of an attractive young woman. Her black, rather wiry, hair is parted on the crown, whence it waves over the sides of the head and streams down behind the neck, one of the curls encroaching upon the right shoulder. The complexion is of ivory whiteness, faintly suffused with rose on the cheeks, while the lips are carmine, and the eyes, which gaze at the spectator, are hazel-brown. The shoulders and bust are nude, save for a bit of yellow-green drapery which the girl holds over her bosom with the left hand.

Signed at the upper right, "G. Max, Susanne."

JEAN LOUIS ERNEST MEISSONIER

FRENCH (1815-1891)

No. 248— JOUEUR DE BOULES, ANTIBES

PANEL

Height, 5¼ inches; width, 4 inches

THE sketch is a record of one of the artist's visits to the picturesque town of Antibes, on the Mediterranean coast, between Nice and Cannes. It is made on a panel of polished wood, the grain of which is exposed, except where the figure is painted. The latter represents a man of sturdy build, facing in profile toward the right, as he stands with the left foot slightly advanced. His rubicund face, furnished with graying side-whiskers, is surmounted by a white hat that is trimmed with a brown band. The man is in his shirt-sleeves, dressed in creamy-white trousers and a drab waistcoat, at the armhole of which appears a glimpse of his yellow suspenders. His hands are held behind his back, as he grasps two bowls, preparatory to rolling them.

Stamped at the back, "VENTE MEISSONIER, 1893."
Signed at the lower right, "E. M."

JEAN LOUIS ERNEST MEISSONIER

FRENCH (1815-1891)

No. 249— LA VIEILLE FEMME FILEUSE, ANTIBES

PANEL

Height. 7 inches; width, 5 inches

THE sketch is executed on a panel of polished wood. It represents an old peasant woman of Antibes, seated facing three-quarters to the right. A distaff is fixed under her left arm and her hands are disposed in the gesture of spinning. Her head is covered with a cap which runs back to a peak and is furnished with flounces over the ears. She wears a pale blue handkerchief, dotted with white, fastened round her neck. The sleeves and body of the gown are merely indicated by reddish shadows, the skirt being touched in sketchily with white. Meanwhile the rendering of the apron has been carried further, the folds being developed in tones of olive drab.

Stamped at the back, "Vente Meissonier."
Signed at the lower left, "E. M."

EUGÈNE BOUDIN

FRENCH (1825-1898)

No. 250— QUAI DE LA DOUANE, VENISE

PANEL

Height, 12½ inches; width, 9 inches

SEEN beyond the foreground of water, the Custom House Quay extends from some brown-roofed buildings at the left nearly across the middle distance. A picturesque tangle of shipping is moored in front of it. The mass includes some barges with single masts, from one of which flies a gray flag with a touch of scarlet, and an ocean-going, square-rigged craft, against whose black hull shows the top of a green mooring post. Alongside the larger vessel lies a barge with a man in the end of it, who seems to be hailing a rowboat, containing a seated and a standing figure. In the distance at the right are indications of buildings, under a gray, weathery sky.

Signed and dated at the lower left, "Venise, '98, E. BOUDIN."

MLLE. ROSA MARIE BONHEUR

FRENCH (1822-1899)

No. 251—

A MOUNTAIN DONKEY

Height, 13 inches; width, 9½ inches

AGAINST a background of bright green mountain, which is succeeded by another of violet green hue, a reddish-brown donkey, of Spanish breed, stands three-quarters in view, facing away from the spectator. The beast's head is free of gear; but on its back is a rosy scarlet saddle, furnished front and rear with a padded roll. Stirrup irons hang from it and a red strap passes round the quarters under the tail. Over the root of the latter lies an ornament, composed of scarlet string and fringe. The head is seen against a shaded hollow in the mountain's side.

Stamped on the back, "VENTE ROSA BONHEUR."
Signed at the lower right, "ROSA BONHEUR."

EMILIO SANCHEZ-PERRIER

SPANISH (-1907)

No. 252—   RIVER LANDSCAPE

PANEL

Height, 10¾ inches; length, 14 inches

PALE blue water whitened with reflections of the sky, spreads from the right
of the foreground and indents irregularly the ground which occupies the left
of the composition.   At the edge of the water a woman, seated in a rectangular
box, is washing laundry.   Two pieces are spread near her.   In the middle
distance a couple of washerwomen appear hard by a group of four, whose
costumes comprise spots of lavender and geranium-red.   The riverside which
is of sand, stony and sprinkled with rushy growth, is bounded in the rear by
a gray hedge of willows, over the top of which rise some trees with yellow
foliage.

Signed at the lower left, "E. SANCHEZ-PERRIER."

JEAN LOUIS ERNEST MEISSONIER

FRENCH (1815-1891)

No. 253—   ESQUISSE D'UNE TROUPE

PANEL

Height, 5 inches; length, 8 inches

A DRAB road, sketchily rendered, leads back diagonally from the right of the foreground. It surmounts an embankment which is indicated at the left by pale blue and green brush-strokes over an underpainting of reddish buff. A single horseman approaches on a bay mount. He is distinguished by a scarlet tunic. Behind him ride a couple of troopers, respectively on a white and dark brown charger. These are followed by the rest of the troop, riding two and two. One of them, mounted on a white horse, is apparently carrying the colors. The sky is sapphire-blue, crossed by fleecy rollers of dove-gray.

*Stamped on the back, "*VENTE MEISSONIER.*"*
Signed at the lower right, "E. M."

LUIGI CHIALIVA

ITALIAN (1842-   )

No. 254—   SHEPHERDESS

Height, 14 inches; width, 10¾ inches

In the foreground a shepherdess faces us, as she stands with her left hand, holding a stick, resting on her hip and the forefinger and thumb of the other hand placed upon the forehead of a black-and-tan dog. Her chestnut hair is partly covered with a bluish-white cap, while her figure is clad in a drab cloak with olive-yellow collar, a lavender body, dull blue apron and dull salmon-colored petticoat. Her sheep are dispersed around her, conspicuous at the right being an ewe with her lamb nestling at her side. In the rear appears a man on horseback, stooping to talk to a girl.

Signed at the lower left, "L. CHIALIVA."

EUGÈNE BOUDIN

FRENCH (1825-1898)

No. 255— TROUVILLE

PANEL

Height, 9½ inches; length, 12¾ inches

FROM the left, where there are indications of buildings overhung with soft masses of green trees, a quay extends back diagonally to the middle distance, where a metal bridge of two s p a n s crosses horizontally to the right. The quay-side is crowded with sailing barges, whose dark brown and olive-drab hulls are reflected in the foreground of water, along with a little blue from the upper sky. Conspicuous amidst the confusion is a white sail, over the top of which appears a spot of rose. Farther back a large hull displays a green band round the gunwale. At the right of it two gray mooring posts rise above the water. Beyond the bridge are visible drab and white sails and the square yards of a vessel. White masses of cloud float above the pale, dove-gray horizon.

Signed at the lower left, "Eug. BOUDIN, Trouville."

WILLEM MARIS

HOLLAND (1844-1910)

No. 256—   PASTURE AND COWS

Height, 10 inches; length, 12¾ inches

THE water in the foreground is broken up with tones of silvery-gray, violet, amber and rosy lavender, and tinged with the red and yellow reflections of two cows. These are standing on a point of land that projects from the right, covered with scrubby long grass, yellowish-green, passing here and there into tones of amber and red. Near the extremity a dark brown cow, with a crimson glow on her hip, stands facing away from the spectator. At her right stands in profile a yellow cow with white muzzle and belly, the top of her back catching the light. The water extends back at the left to a white line, above which are indications of a windmill and woods. The cool blue sky is scattered with creamy vapor, which has settled thick above the horizon.

Signed at the lower left, "WILLEM MARIS."

JOHANNES HENDRIK WEISSENBRUCH

HOLLAND (1824-1903)

No. 257—   THE CANAL NEAR BASKOP

PANEL

Height, 8 inches; length, 15¼ inches

THE white clouds that cluster in the center of the sky are reflected in the canal which stretches directly back from the foreground. The surface is also dyed with patches of pale green and darkened at its edges with the shadow of the banks. On the right a row of willows with soft yellow foliage extends back to one of dark olive hue. Where the canal disappears from sight a woman, in black gown and white cap, is stooping to the ground near two tubs, containing laundry. At the left of the foreground a brown cottage, with white frames round the windows and a wooden leader from its thatched roof, is seen behind three tall willows.

Signed at the lower right, "H. WEISSENBRUCH."

JOHAN BARTHOLD JONGKIND

HOLLAND (1822-1891)

No. 258—   MOONLIGHT ON A CANAL

Height, 13 inches; length, 17 inches

THE surface of the canal, stretching back from the foreground, is mottled with the reflections of a swirl of creamy and slaty purple clouds that surround the full moon. It is also shaded by the dark hulls and tangle of masts, yards and ropes of barges, moored alongside a quay at the right. Here appears the entrance to a side canal, in front of which rises a tall, straight stem that forks out at the top and spreads its scanty foliage against the pale blue of this part of the sky. At the back of the water a windmill rears aloft near a house that is distinguished by a large window, illumined with a red glow.

Signed and dated at the lower right, "JONGKIND, '68."

WILLEM MARIS

HOLLAND (1844-1910)

No. 259--   GOOSE AND GOSLINGS

Height, 18½ inches; width, 14 inches

OVER the juicy yellow-green grass of the foreground a white goose is conducting her brood of tiny goslings. Three precede her, while five are clustered in her wake, two others being still in the water, which crosses the middle distance. The surface is dyed with lavender-purple and the yellow reflections of the large leaves which overhang the pond. They sprinkle the limbs of some trees that are seen against a farther mass of dense brown foliage. The latter discloses at the top a peep of blue sky. At the left of the foreground, with her blue head tucked close between her shoulders, sits a duck.

Signed at the lower left, "WILLEM MARIS."

JACOB MARIS

HOLLAND (1838-1899)

No. 260— A PINK ON SHORE AT SCHEVENINGEN

A HOLLAND "pink," its creamy-yellow sail lowered nearly to the gunwale, lies beached in the foreground. Blue, white and red stripes decorate the tip of her mast, from which a red pennon flies. The bow shows the painted device of a gray semicircle, marked with two blue chevrons. A cart is drawn up alongside, with a white horse in the shafts. The driver is dressed in yellow oilskins. The olive-buff and greenish coloring of the boat's hull is reflected on the damp sand, which elsewhere is broken up into tones of silvery drab.

Signed at the lower right, "J. MARIS."   *Height, 19 inches; width, 16 inches.*
Collection of N. W. Van Delden, Amsterdam.

ARTHUR HOEBER, A. N. A.

AMERICAN (1854-   )

No. 261—   THE SEA

Height, 14 inches; length, 22 inches

A HEAVE of water, sliding across the middle distance, lobs up at the left to a white crest, and along its line is flicked into lesser points.   Its hue of greenish-blue is streaked with cream and faint rose and lavender.   The horizon is suffused with primrose-drab vapor, slightly tinged with rose.

Signed at the lower left, "ARTHUR HOEBER."

ARTHUR HOEBER, A. N. A.

AMERICAN (1854-   )

No. 262—   UPON A SUMMER'S DAY

Height, 25 inches; length 30 inches

ACROSS the foreground extends a rude wall of rocks, greenish-gray and amber in the light, and in the shadows violet and bluish.   Beyond this extends the green, faintly blue, sea, interrupted in the distance at the right by a schooner with white sails, one with her masts bare, and a boat with a single sail.   Layers of creamy cloud bar the pale blue sky, which deepens to slate at the right.

Signed at the lower right, "ARTHUR HOEBER."

HENRI REGNAULT

FRENCH (1843-1871)

No. 263— THE HEAD OF AN ARAB

Height, 18¾ inches; width, 16 inches

THE swarthy face, reddish-brown, gray and glossy in the high lights, wears a black moustache and short, thin, curling beard around the cheeks and chin. The head is very slightly inclined to the left, the eyes looking down. A whitish drab cloth covers the crown, a touch of yellow showing over the black curls at the left, while behind the hair at the right hangs a golden creamy neck-covering. A little of the pale, slaty-gray robe appears at the base of the long neck. The whole is sketchily but vividly rendered against a white background.

Sedelmeyer stamped on the back.
Signed at the lower right. "À mon ami, VAYSON, H. R."
From the E. Lyon Collection, Paris, 1903.

ADELBERT CUYP

HOLLAND (1605-1691)

No. 264—   LADY AND HORSE

PANEL

Height, 14½ inches; width, 11½ inches

A DAPPLE-GRAY palfrey, with scarlet ribbons hanging from the sides of his bridle, occupies the center of the foreground. He stands beside a lady who turns her head to look at him, as she sits on a mounting-block at the left. Her hair is decorated with a jewel from which a rose and a gold scarf hangs, the ends being crossed over her bosom. Her body is encased in a short-sleeved, tight-fitting tunic, like a cuirass, of pale creamy green and rose striped material. A rose-colored drapery covers her lap, on which her right hand rests, while an orange-tawny and white spaniel, standing on his hind legs, licks it. In the shadow behind the lady a negro holds a crimson cloak, bunched on his head. Elevated in the rear are a statue of a figure, clad in a toga, and a terminal surmounted by the wreathed head of Priapus.

Black seal on the back.

Signed at the lower right, "A. CUYP."

PIETER BREUGHEL, THE ELDER

FLEMISH (1525-1569)

No. 265—   LANDSCAPE WITH CANAL

PANEL

Height, 18 inches; length, 29 inches

A CANAL stretches from the left of the foreground to a single-arch bridge, furnished with a toll-house, in the middle distance. Near its right extremity stands a red-gabled tavern, in front of which appear a hooded wagon and a crowd of people. In the immediate foreground on this side a woman is seated in a cart drawn by a single horse, on which a man is riding. Among the figures which animate the front plane, and present in their costumes hues of scarlet, blue, gray and olive, are three men, toward the left of the center, who are forking what looks like hay into a wagon. Sail boats are drawn up on the edge of the canal while in midstream is a ferry-boat, laden with cows.

JACOB VAN RUISDAEL

HOLLAND (1628-1682)

No. 266— LANDSCAPE WITH FIGURES

Height, 29 inches; width, 25½ inches.

A LOG lies across the left of the foreground. A few feet back some bushes grow at the base of a greenish-brown oak trunk, with corrugated bark, which leans slightly to the left. Near it is another, with grayish-green stem, similarly inclined. In front of it a man is seated with his back to us. He is dressed in a black felt hat, a buff coat, and high boots with scarlet flaps. Beside him, on a roadway, stands another man whose costume comprises a drab hat, dark green belted coat, red stockings and white flaps to his boots. Farther back in the roadway, in the shadow of some trees on a knoll at the left, a figure in black approaches.

An imperfect signature near the log suggests, "Ruisdael, fct."

JAN MONCHABLON

FRENCH (1855-1903)

No. 267—　　　VUE DE CHÂTILLONS, VOSGES

Height, 15 inches; length, 22 inches

An elongated triangle of very yellow herbage, sprinkled with a little green vegetation and some small boulders, stretches across the foreground from the right. Its diagonal line is paralleled by a pinkish-brown strip of newly plowed soil, at the right extremity of which a shepherdess and her flock are seen in front of a wall that fronts a shed. The parallelism is continued by a strip of green, where some cows are feeding. After this the ground, broken up into patches of cultivation, slopes up to an eminence, crowned by a village of red-roofed houses. Above them rises a tower, surmounted by a spire.

Signed and dated at the lower right, "JAN MONCHABLON, 1891."

JEAN FRANÇOIS RAFFAELLI

FRENCH (1850-   )

No. 268—   LE CHIFFONIER

PANEL

Height, 19 inches; width, 13¾ inches

THE rag-picker sits three-quarters to the right on the rim of a tall basket, balancing his body by resting his right hand on the opposite edge. Behind him, at the left, is a bank of sandy soil, tufted with scanty vegetation, while at the right the low ground extends back along a sheet of water, the monotony of which is broken by a small boat. Across the water are indications of a red roof and a factory smokestack. A black soft felt hat covers the man's head, which is turned to the spectator, revealing a face shaggy with brown side-whiskers and beard and a moustache and patch under the lower lip of buff color. Round his neck is knotted a blue handkerchief; the rest of his attire consisting of an olive-slaty coat over a white shirt, a pair of bluish-yellow trousers and low shoes.

Signed at the lower left, "J. F. RAFFAELLI."

FÉLIX ZIEM

No. 269— PUBLIC GARDENS, VENICE, MOONLIGHT

FRENCH (1821-1911)

Height, 16½ inches; length, 25 inches

A SECTION of the parapet of the Public Gardens of Venice projects from the left of the middle distance, interrupted near the center of the composition by the steps and balustrades of the water entrance. The trees of the garden present masses of golden-brown tones which are reflected in the deep blue water that reaches to the foreground. Toward greenish-blue mooring posts, grouped near the landing, a black-hooded gondola is approaching. Two passengers are visible, one of them being distinguished by a white headdress and a scarlet cloak. Another gondola, with a red light attached to the front of its hood, is crossing to the right, cleaving the dripping reflections of a waning moon that hangs in gray vapor over the brown shore of the Lido. The upper sky at the left is blue, diagonally streaked with cirrus.

Signed at the lower left, "ZIEM."

ARTHUR HOEBER, A. N. A.

AMERICAN (1854-   )

No. 270—   THE FLOWING TIDE

Height, 22 inches; length, 30 inches

In the middle distance, at the right, the square-rigged sails of a vessel, and, near to the center, the still farther sail of a fishing boat, loom phantom-like against the faint lavender vapor which is banked over the horizon. Above it emerges the upper half of a full moon. Its reflections form a path to the front, where the greenish-gray sea becomes pale sapphire, mottled with rose and lavender, as it winds its way over the sandy foreground.

Signed at the lower right, "ARTHUR HOEBER."

ARTHUR HOEBER, A. N. A.

AMERICAN (1854-   )

No. 271—   WOODLAND SOLITUDE

Height, 25 inches; length, 30 inches

The water, at the right of the foreground, is striped with the olive-green reflections of some oaks which are clustered on a projecting point of ground. A smaller point at the left is distinguished by three tree-trunks, growing close together. In the rear the pool is bounded by a horizontal screen of woodland, where the foliage glows with yellow light, as if there were an opening beyond.

Signed at the lower left, "ARTHUR HOEBER."

ÉMILE VAN MARCKE

FRENCH (1827-1890)

No. 272—   SHEEP IN THE PASTURE

PANEL

Height, 7¾ inches; length, 10 inches

THREE sheep are lying in the foreground of a pasture, the one at the right being half in shadow. Behind the other two stands a blackish-brown sheep, at the left of which a white one is feeding, its body seen in profile, enveloped in shadow. The field is bounded in the middle distance by a horizontal line of fence, about the center of which rises a young tree, bushy with yellow foliage. At the right of it a man in a sapphire-blue blouse leans on the top rail, talking to a woman in a white cap and rosy bodice, who stands on the farther side of the fence. The shepherd's black dog has left him and is racing toward the right.

Signed at the lower right, "ÉM. VAN MARCKE."

CONSTANT TROYON

FRENCH (1813-1865)

No. 273—   SHEEP IN THE PASTURE

PANEL

Height, 13 inches; width, 10 inches

THE face of a sheep, lying beside another in the foreground, catches the light and forms the focus point of a scheme of golden yellow-brown tonality. At the left of the foreground a stick lies on the grass beside a dark green bush. Over the top of the latter appears the back of a sheep, seen in profile, which is paralleled by another. A fifth sheep stands, cropping the grass, at the right; while still another faces us, lying down at the back of the scene.

A seal at the back, also a statement in writing, "I guarantee this painting an original work by C. Troyon.—WILLIAM SCHAUS."

Signed at the lower left, "C. TROYON."

ÉMILE VAN MARCKE

FRENCH (1827-1890)

No. 274— CATTLE RETURNING HOME

PANEL

Height, 8½ inches; width, 12½ inches

A ROADWAY, marked with ruts and bordered with deep green stubbly grass, curves back from the center of the foreground. It leads back to a belt of sandy soil that cuts the composition horizontally. Above the edge of it appear the upper parts of two cows and of a woman in white cap and pale blue garment, as they descend the opposite side. The woman is followed by other cows which are fully visible, the procession being concluded by a woman who bends beneath the load of a faggot. She is seen at the left of a willow that has greenish-brown foliage, growing from a dark olive trunk which reflects a little gray light. At the right of the foreground is a stretch of buff, overgrown with some tall reedlike growth. The sky is gray, with one globule of light, floating over a few streaks.

Signed at the lower left, "ÉM. VAN MARCKE."

CHARLES ÉMILE JACQUE

FRENCH (1813-1894)

No. 275—   FEEDING TIME

Height, 18½ inches; width, 15¼ inches

In the foreground of the stable a black cock with a wealth of gold feathers around his throat stands proudly among his hens. Some are picking at what appears to be bright yellow corn, while a reddish hen and a gray one are attacking some curly cabbage leaves which lie near a drinking trough. Meanwhile, as if in response to the cock's summons, two hens are hurrying down a ladder, which leads to an upper door at the right; the foremost bird having sprung into mid air with extended wings. The angle of the stable walls is wreathed with cobwebs, at the left of which a lantern hangs beside a small window, the sill of which is strewn with straw.

Signed at the lower left, "Ch. Jacque."

ANTOINE VOLLON

FRENCH (1833-1900)

No. 276—   THE FISHERMAN'S RETURN

Height, 18 inches; length, 22 inches

A FISHERMAN and his little child, followed by the wife carrying a basket, advance to the front along a roadway that leads directly from the sea. The latter shows in a pale blue band between the cottages which flank the extremity of the road. At the right appears a gable end, above which a flock of gulls is flying. Adjoining it is an olive-brown thatched roof, cut by a rose-red chimney. Another chimney rises at the left beside a bit of reddish-brown roof and a creamy white gable that catches the light. They show above a mass of greenery. The sky is of robin's egg blue, silted over with a little sooty vapor.

Signed at the lower left, "A. VOLLON."

EUGÈNE FROMENTIN

FRENCH (1820-1876)

No. 277—   HUNTING WITH FALCONS

Height, 15½ inches, length, 26½ inches

THREE mounted Arabs are stationed at the right of the foreground, on the edge of a shallow marsh which occupies the middle distance. Here, toward the left, a horseman is coming forward at the gallop with hand upraised, as he follows the course of two falcons which are hovering above a heron. Farther back, another rider gallops forward and other horsemen are dotted around the edge of the swamp. The leader of the group in the foreground, wearing a white burnoos and swathed about the body with scarlet, is mounted on a lavender-roan steed. At the right of him, his back to the spectator, an attendant, with a falcon on his shoulder, sits a blue roan, while facing us is another, mounted on a dove-colored horse, who holds a bird on his uplifted wrist.

Signed at the lower left, "EUG. FROMENTIN."

ÉMILE VAN MARCKE

FRENCH (1827-1890)

No. 278—   THE PASTURE—EVENING

Height, 20 inches; length, 25¾ inches

In the foreground of the pasture a pale reddish cow, marked with creamy white, stands a trifle inclined from the front, but turning her head to the spectator. One horn shows against the rich red-brown coat of another cow, as she looks back toward a brown with white face and chest which stands in the middle distance. Still farther back a yellow cow is lying under a tree which crowns the slope of the pasture at the right. Over at the left of the summit is a continuous mass of amber-brown foliage. A blackberry bush with white blossoms occupies the right of the foreground.

Signed and dated at the lower right, "Ém. Van Marcke, '69."

ANTOINE VOLLON

FRENCH (1833-1900)

No. 279—   STILL LIFE

Height, 24 inches; width, 19½ inches

On a plain deal table, partly covered by a green drapery, is disposed a white china bowl, containing two very large yellow pears and an orange. These are flanked by some amber grapes, while a bunch of purple ones lies at the right. Behind it stands a gilt embossed flagon with a wide, flaring lip, at the left of which appears a deep blue bottle-shaped vase of Oriental ware. The objects are seen against an orange tawny brown and greenish background.

Signed at the lower left, "A. Vollon."

JULES DUPRÉ

FRENCH (1812-1889)

No. 280—   THE POND

PANEL

Height, 6¾ inches; length, 9 inches

A POND extends back from the right of the foreground. On the bank at the left two scarlet spots show against a bunch of reeds or shaggy grass; and farther back a brown mass is visible at the foot of an oak. The latter, which has several splintered limbs, leans toward the pond. Two cows, a dark red and a rosy and white one, are standing in the water near the rushy bank at the right. Here a horizontal strip of light green meadow stretches to a clump of rich dark trees in the middle distance. They are massed against a blue horizon, over which float bold volumes of white and gray-blue cloud, under a canopy of dove-gray.

Signed at the lower left, "JULES DUPRÉ."
From the Jules Cronier Collection, 1908, No. 31.

JEAN BAPTISTE CAMILLE COROT

FRENCH (1796-1875)

No. 281— MORNING

Height, 10 inches; length, 19 inches

THE foreground of mossy yellow-green pasture, sprinkled with a few yellow flowers, extends to a band of whitish water which lies horizontally across the middle distance. It is bounded on the farther side by woods, lavender-gray against the grayish-creamy vapor that hovers over the horizon. The sky above is clearing to a faint gray-blue. Massed against it at the left is the softly blurred, yellow-olive-gray foliage of a bunch of three willows which occupy the foreground on this side. Against the trunk of one of them leans a woman whose costume includes the suggestion of a red cape and a whitish apron over a drab petticoat. Her cows are strung along the waterside. A red and a white one are turned toward the right; a red with white head faces us, and a black, whose body is toward the water, looks round to the front.

Signed at the lower right, "Corot."

JULES DUPRÉ

FRENCH (1811-1889)

No. 282—   MORNING

ON the left bank of a pool extending back from the right of the foreground
stands an oak.   The white light catches its trunk and some of the boughs.
These grow out of a bunch of deep green foliage and are scantily fledged with
yellowish-brown leafage, touched with rose at the top.   A willow grows on a
spit of bank that projects from the right.   Here a punt lies, with a man in
it whose cap and shirt reflect the light sharply.   Large white clouds float over
the horizon in a blue sky.

Signed at the lower left, "JULES DUPRE."   *Height, 16 inches; width, 13 inches.*

CHARLES FRANÇOIS DAUBIGNY

FRENCH (1817-1878)

No. 283— RIVER LANDSCAPE—HARVEST MOON

PANEL

Height, 14¾ inches; length, 26½ inches

THE bluish-green water, reflecting the orange-yellow hues of a harvest moon, appears within a horseshoe of bank. The latter sweeps boldly down from the right across the foreground, terminating in a reedy spit. At the summit of the slope a poplar rises out of a clump of rich green foliage. Adjoining it, at the left, is another eminence, covered with a group of cottages, one of which has white walls and a rosy roof. From this point the line of bank, brushed in with vigorous strokes, crosses horizontally to the left, where, between the stems of some trees, the moon shows. In a little rushy inlet in the center of the foreground, two black ducklings are swimming. Three white and brown ones are approaching the water, while a black hen stands half-way up the slope.

Signed at the lower right, "DAUBIGNY."

NARCISSE VIRGILE DIAZ DE LA PEÑA

FRENCH (1802-1876)

No. 284—   EDGE OF THE FOREST

PANEL

Height, 26 inches; length, 30½ inches

THE foreground presents an open space, covered with soft loose yellowish grass. It is interrupted on the left by three boulders, one of which reflects the light, while a pocket of water in the center of the front catches a glint of blue sky. From it straggles back a footpath, along which a woman in bluish-purple skirt and old rose cap approaches, bending under the weight of a faggot. The upper part of her figure shows against a white pool of water, beyond which a stretch of yellow grass extends to some trees. These are silhouetted against the blue horizon, over which float smoky masses of white vapor. This central interval is flanked on each side, in the middle distance, by a bunch of young oaks, fledged with yellow-green. In advance of the one on the left stands a single oak with brownish trunk and a sprinkle of leaves.

Signed and dated at the lower left, "N. DIAZ, '71."
From the Henry Graves Collection, 1909.

JULES DUPRÉ

FRENCH (1811-1889)

No. 285—   THE OLD OAK

Height, 41 inches; length, 41 inches

THE golden brown tonality, which envelopes the ground and trees, also pervades
the sky. In the center of the foreground an oak with splintered limbs leans
over to the left, its trunk being crossed low down by another from which the
top is broken.   A fallen tree lies on the ground behind the oak, and another
is stretched across the left of the foreground.   The clearing is bounded at the
back by forest.   Its density is interrupted in the center by some light, while
at the left appears the vista of an irregular avenue.

Signed at the lower left, "J. DUPRE."

HENRI LEROLLE

FRENCH (1851-   )

No. 286—   REAPERS NEAR VERSAILLES

Height, 26 inches; length, 32 inches

In the evening glow two women are working in the harvest field. One is upon her knees at the left of the foreground, binding a sheaf of wheat. Her brown hair is uncovered and, as she stoops, her broad bosom shows from the loose chemise. A drab-gray skirt completes her attire. In the center of the composition a pile of sheaves and two separate sheaves, lying beside it, are warmly illuminated to an orange-tawny hue. Behind the mass stands another woman, bending slightly to the left. She holds a sickle in her right hand, while on her left arm lies a small bunch of wheat. Other piles of sheaves dot the stubble field. In the distance a ridge of purple hills extends horizontally beneath the dove-gray horizon, which is barred with sweeps of rosy yellow.

Signed at the lower right, "H. LEROLLE."

HENRI HARPIGNIES

FRENCH (1819-   )

No. 287—   THE BROOK

Height, 32 inches; width, 25¾ inches.

A BROOK, streaked with blue and white reflections, comes sliding down between mossy banks to the left of the foreground.   On the left bank, side by side, are two tall trees, clothed at the top with tufts of foliage that show softly against the blue of the upper sky.   The ground behind them slopes up to the left, its edge being interrupted by two bushes.   In the middle distance stands a young birch, which is crossed at the back by a thicker trunk, wreathed with ivy.

Signed and dated at the left of the lower center, "H. HARPIGNIES, 1900."

JEAN CHARLES CAZIN

FRENCH (1840-1900)

No. 288—   THE THAW

Height, 32½ inches; length, 39½ inches

THE desolate foreground is tufted with grayish-buff tussets of dead growth, between which the snow has partially melted, discovering patches of yellow-green mossy grass. At the extreme right is a square pile of what may be stones, overtopped by a scraggy bush. The dunes recede to a long level reach of elevated ground, on which, as it begins to slope down at the right, appears an obelisk or lighthouse. The slope, in the intervals between the snow, is colored, variously, green and sapphire-blue, fawn and cream. The only sign of life is eight birds flying at the left of the rosy drab sky.

Signed at the lower right, "J. C. CAZIN."

CHARLES ÉMILE JACQUE

FRENCH (1813-1894)

No. 289—   THE SHEPHERD

Height, 32 inches; width, 25¾ inches.

THE light sprinkles the silvery trunks and filters through the foliage of three oaks which occupy a knoll where a shepherd is watching his flock. Clad in a soft drab hat, pale blue blouse and olive-green trousers, the man stands in front of the middle tree, leaning forward onto his stick. His dog sits with his back to the spectator, watching three yearling lambs, one of which eyes him cautiously. Other sheep are scattered over the summit, which is enclosed with oaks.

Signed and dated at the lower left, "CH. JACQUE, '75."
From the Dr. Fournier Collection, Paris.

MADAME MARIE DIÉTERLE

FRENCH (1860-   )

No. 290—   L'ETANG DE JOBE, NORMANDIE

Height, 30¾ inches; length, 40½ inches

THE rushy water of the pool fills the foreground. In the center of it stands, three-quarters to the left, a handsome, rather shaggy, brown-red cow, with a white face and a white spot on her back. Under her head appears the white face, lowered to the water, of a reddish-yellow cow. Farther back, near the bank, a yellow calf stands in advance of a fawn cow and beside a white one. The background at the left is enclosed with loosely massed foliage of a faint green, changing to dove-gray as the trees recede.

Signed at the lower right, "MARIE DIETERLE."

ADOLF SCHREYER

GERMAN (1828-1899)

No. 291—   ARAB RIDERS

PANEL

Height, 24 inches; length, 44¾ inches

An Arab cavalcade has reached a drinking fountain, and in the center of the foreground a black horse, glistening with coppery and purplish tones, has lowered his head into the large square water-basin. The rider, seated on a yellow saddle, embellished with scarlet, is swathed in white, with a rosy pink sash round the waist and a yellow band confining his head-wrap. At the left of the fountain the standard-bearer, holding a white and green flag, has dismounted from his chestnut; while at the right of the basin a man in a scarlet and yellow turban stands beside a creamy-white and dapple-gray mount. In the middle distance, at the extreme right, two pack horses are approaching in charge of a Nubian in a red fez, who is mounted on one of them. An eminence in the rear of the fountain is occupied by a cluster of buildings, surmounted by a flat dome.

Signed at the lower right, "Ad. Schreyer."

LÉON AUGUSTIN LHERMITTE

FRENCH (1844-   )

No. 292—   THE REAPER'S LUNCH

Height, 33 inches; length, 43½ inches

IN the center of the foreground of stubble, which is dotted in the rear with piles of wheat-sheaves, a young reaper is raising a pitcher to his lips. His figure, which is seen in profile, arched back, with the head held high, is clad in a bright straw hat, white shirt and pale blue trousers that are streaked with silvery tones. The man faces a young woman in a pinkish-cream sunbonnet, who is seated at his right on a sheaf, upon which her right hand rests, as she looks toward the back of the field. On the lap of her blue skirt lies her baby, holding up its hands to the mother's breast, which the chemisette exposes. At the woman's feet a little dark haired girl, dressed in a skirt striped with two tones of fawn, lies on her stomach beside a gray pot.

Signed and dated at the lower left, "LHERMITTE," 1890."

THÉOPHILE DE BOCK

HOLLAND (1851-1904)

No. 293—   MILKING TIME NEAR VOORBURG

Height, 47½ inches; width, 32¼ inches.

A BROWNISH-DRAB road curves round to the right of a pool to an open gate
in the middle distance.   Some cows are approaching it, followed by a milkmaid
who carries a brass pitcher.   She wears a white cap, olive-black bodice with
drab-olive sleeves and a blue apron.

Signed at the lower right, "THEOPHILE DE BOCK."

JOHANNES HENDRIK WEISSENBRUCH

HOLLAND (1824-1903)

No. 294—   ON THE SHORE

Height, 40 inches; length, 50½ inches

SOME little way back at the right the foreground of buff-drab sand is cut into
by a pool of shallow water. On the far side of it a drabish-brown two-
wheeled cart, with a white horse in the shafts, is drawn up alongside a fishing
boat, which shows a pale green gunwale over her yellowish-olive hull. Her
boom is lowered and the brown-amber sail reefed to it. A brown vane-bag
flutters from her masthead. The sky is stirred with wind and threatening
storm; the gray of the horizon being piled with blusters of creamy buff,
opening to a flare of cream.

Signed and dated at the lower right, "J. H. WEISSENBRUCH, 20 Oct., 1901."

JOSEF ISRAËLS

HOLLAND (1824-1911)

No. 295—　　　　　　DOMESTIC TROUBLE

Height, 38½ inches; length, 52 inches

A YOUNG wife sits disconsolately before a fireless hearth at the left of the foreground, while in the rear of the kitchen at the right her husband is drinking and playing cards with two cronies. She leans her face against her left hand, while the right, with a knife in it, lies on the potatoes in a green earthenware pan on her lap. She has an air of extreme orderliness and much refinement. A brown cloth protects her scarlet apron and drab skirt. Her bodice is made of pretty material, with broad stripes of rosy cream and blue, and her dainty cap of white lawn with a net border, edged with lace, shows at the neck a fringe of soft blond hair. The light plays over the sad expression of her fresh-colored face. The husband is dressed in fisherman's clothes: blue woollen cap and a brown blouse over a scarlet jersey.

Signed at the lower left, "J. ISRAELS."
From the Du Bois Collection, Amsterdam, 1907.

FELIX ZIEM

FRENCH (1821-1911)

No. 296—   VIEW OF CONSTANTINOPLE

Height, 42 inches; length, 63½ inches

SEEN across the water, as it extends back from the foreground, lies a steamer
with dark funnel and three square-rigged masts, from which hang streamers of
blue, rose and yellow bunting. The opposite shore presents a horizontal vista
of golden-yellow buildings, above which, at the right, soar the dome and four
minarets of S. Sophia, gleaming white against the sky. The scene on this
side is framed in with a thicket of masts and sails, in front of which a man in
red coat is rowing a skiff. From the left of the foreground, where there is an
irregularly indented brown shore, a long boat filled with gaily dressed figures,
one of whom offers the contrast of white, is being propelled by three rowers.
In the distance at the left the skyline is interrupted by a minaret and mosque.
The sky is of pale robin's-egg blue, sprinkled with fleecy clouds of rosy cream.

Signed at the lower left, "ZIEM."

MADAME MARIE DIÉTERLE

FRENCH (1860-   )

No. 297—   LA REINE DU TROUPEAU

Height, 45½ inches; length, 65½ inches

THE queen of the herd, a beautiful creamy white, varied with lavender-rosy tones, stands at the right of the foreground, with one foot in some reedy water. The latter is a bit of the sea, which shows in the rear, dotted with two sailboats. Above the cow's back appear the purplish-brown forehead and horns of another cow, whose stern is also visible in shadow. In front of it stands a yellow calf with white forehead, facing us; while to its left is another, brown and white, which stands beside a cow similarly colored, but in richer hues. Other cows are grouped farther back at the left, where a man in blue blouse is seated on a bareback, bridleless horse, apparently shouting to the remainder of the herd, which is straggling up from some lower ground.

Signed at the lower left, "DIETERLE."

ARTHUR HOEBER, A. N. A.

AMERICAN (1854-   )

No. 298—   HYANNIS PORT, MOONLIGHT

Height, 16 inches; length, 30 inches

REFLECTING, at the right, the hues of a full moon that hangs in primrose vapor, the smooth water stretches back from the front in tones of green and sapphire. In the middle distance at the left, a level shore or wharf lies along the horizon. Near the end of it a point of yellow light shows on a pole, while another appears farther to the left, amid indications of buildings A steamboat lies off the shore, and nearer to the front is a fishing schooner, with her lavender sails set.

Signed at the lower right, "ARTHUR HOEBER."

ARTHUR HOEBER, A. N. A.

AMERICAN (1854-   )

No. 299—   RESTLESS SEA

Height, 25 inches; length, 30 inches

A WAVE is shown diagonally across the middle distance, traveling to the right, with a frill of white overhanging its green hollow. In front of it, as the ripples scurry forward, their greens pass in and out of dark and light and are tinged with buff, whitish-gray and lavender-pink. Over a horizon choked with greenish-slaty vapor, the sky is stirred with primrose and flecked with pale violet and amber clouds.

Signed and dated at the lower left, "ARTHUR HOEBER, 1907."

LIST OF ARTISTS REPRESENTED AND
THEIR WORK

LIST OF ARTISTS REPRESENTED AND THEIR WORK

L. M